Ancient Wisdom

Ancient Wisdom

The Book of Proverbs
with Devotions for Today

James MacDonald

B&H
PUBLISHING GROUP

Nashville Tennessee

Dedication

To my prayerful grandmother,
Eileen MacDonald,
who in her lifetime embodied
and promoted the biblical concept of wisdom.

Preface

The Hebrew concept of wisdom is immensely practical. To the Greek, wisdom was to *know!* They considered the accumulation of factual data a worthy end in itself. To the Hebrew, however, wisdom was not in the knowing but in the *doing.*

Solomon knew this.

You'll remember when God appeared to him and said, "Because you've got a lot of responsibility on your shoulders, I'm going to give you any one thing you ask for," this son of the great King David could have wished for anything: long life, wealth, prosperity, you name it. But he knew it wasn't going to be enough just to *have* something. He needed to know how to *do* something—to lead the great nation of Israel.

So he asked God for a heart of wisdom.

This worked out great for us, too, because Solomon's book of Proverbs—which is included in its entirety in the back of this book—reflects God's wisdom on all kinds of things: our marriages, our children, our money, our work, our friendships, and dozens of other topics from everyday life. The wisdom of the Proverbs is "ancient" only in terms of when it was written down. It is old only in its historical and cultural context. In truth, it's as here-and-now as the morning train or the afternoon mail. God's *Ancient Wisdom* is meant for this very moment.

Indeed, the wisest decision a person can make is to receive by faith the offer of eternal life that God extends to us. It's not enough just to know about it. To know and not respond is ultimately the greatest act of foolishness anyone could ever make. If you'd like to learn about and respond to God's offer of salvation, talk to someone you know who is a Christian, or go to www.lifeway.com/salvation. You'll be glad you did.

This book is about *doing* the wisdom of God—30 days of applying God's Word to your life. It's a month of being blessed by the eternal wisdom found only in God's Word. Do what it says and delight yourself in the true wisdom of God's ways.

James MacDonald
Chicago, Illinois

Day 1
Main Thing

Wisdom is supreme—so get wisdom.
And whatever else you get, get understanding.
Proverbs 4:7

Even though the book of Proverbs is more or less a rapid-fire, quick-hitting list of *Ancient Wisdom*, there are key verses inside that sum up the whole thing. This is one of them, and it basically has one message:

Wisdom—*Get it! You'll need it!*

That's because life is made up of choices, and wisdom is essential to making sure those choices are the right ones, the best ones. Who you are today is the sum total of the choices you've made. We could wish this weren't true, especially when things aren't going well, when we want to retreat from the consequences of our own decisions, blaming it on our parents or our upbringing or our spouse or . . . anybody but us.

"This can't be all my fault, can it?"

This practice of shifting blame to others is fueled by those psychologists who make their living endorsing personal memberships in the "Not My Fault Club." They don't seem to agree with people who study these matters carefully and biblically, who tell us that life is 10 percent what happens *to* us, and 90 percent how we choose to deal with it.

We all want to make good, solid choices with every opportunity we have. Therefore, we need wisdom. And we need to go get it!

You can't find true, lasting wisdom just anywhere, so where do you go to get it? All wisdom is God's and comes from God. If you have a thimbleful of wisdom, it's not because you've figured stuff out on your own but because God in his grace has revealed it to you. Any other knowledge we pick up along the way that is not God's wisdom is what the Bible calls the "world's wisdom," which amounts to "foolishness" in God's eyes" (1 Cor. 3:19). It is stupidity by contrast.

Acquire wisdom—how much better it is than gold! And acquire understanding— it is preferable to silver.

PROVERBS 16:16

So let's not get bogged down in the world's wisdom. You'll hear it spouted on afternoon talk shows, at the gym, at the hair place, or on prime-time. Seek after God's wisdom alone, because it's absolutely essential to life.

I like to define wisdom this way: *Wisdom is the best choice with the best result in every situation.* If we build within our heart a passion for wisdom, a hunger and thirst for godly perspective and understanding, we will become increasingly wise—not because we're so smart, but because we're acting as God wants us to.

Get wisdom, Solomon said. "If you find yourself close to it, reach out and grab it. Don't let it pass you by. Stop and listen, then get it for yourself where you can take it home and let it sink into your life."

Get wisdom. "Whatever else you get," make sure this pursuit comes first, learning from God, learning from wise followers of Christ, learning and putting God's wisdom into practice.

Get wisdom. Most of the true wisdom you come across is going to be found in the Bible. Yet many of us spend little time reading the Word of God. If you truly want the ability to make sound decisions and well-placed choices, then invest a lot of time studying, understanding, and listening to God's Word.

Get wisdom, my friend. Get it because God wants to give it. Get it because it's essential to life.

Wisdom Talking

What are some life principles you've been learning lately from God's Word? How are you sharing them with others, with your friends, with your children?

Day 2
Careless Feet

A wise man is cautious and turns from evil,
but a fool is easily angered and is careless.
Proverbs 14:16

In thinking about what makes a wise person truly wise, sometimes it's helpful to point out the contrast—to see what makes a foolish person so obviously foolish.

There are actually three Hebrew words that translate into our English word *fool*. One of them—*eviyl*—(pronounced, ev-EEL) is used nineteen times in the book of Proverbs. This word describes a type of person who's been acting like an idiot for quite some time. A fool of long standing.

This is the kind of guy who never fears until he falls. He just sort of walks through life, never really setting a course for himself, never sensing, "Whoa, that's a little dangerous. Don't want to go over there." He never learns, never seems to remember, "Hey, the last time I went over there, I got really hurt."

You may say, "Well, we all make mistakes in our lives. We all fall." True. I mean, there's nothing that's automatically stupid about making a dumb mistake. We all do that from time to time. It's not blatantly foolish to fail. *It is* foolish, though, to keep choosing the wrong in exactly the same way—over and over again.

That's why we can say a fool is someone with *careless feet*—a man, a woman, a kid, a teenager, who just never seems to get the message that every time they walk this one particular way, they always end up in trouble, in trauma, or in some sort of a mess. They keep going back. And keep going back. And keep making things worse, on themselves and everyone else they inflict along the way.

> A sensible person sees danger and takes cover, but the inexperienced keep going and are punished.
> PROVERBS 22:3

When we see this in children, we sort of understand it. We deal with them rather gently about it. Proverbs 22:15 says, "Foolishness is tangled up in the heart of a youth," so we treat them with patience and care.

Honestly, we adults should know by now—from all the Scriptures we've read, from all the teaching we've heard, from all our personal experience—that certain paths always lead to problems. I've learned, for example, that if I consistently work too many hours and neglect my family, it causes me breakdown and heartache. If I don't make a daily habit of spending time with God in prayer and in his Word—if I'm not careful to take care of my soul—things start to unravel in my life really fast.

We could sit down and name a hundred of these scenarios without thinking hard. Like if we keep our credit cards maxed out to buy this or that thing—or just to cover other debts by moving money around—we're always going to feel like the world is falling in around us. The thrill of buying something is so brief compared to the long months of paying it off, paycheck by paycheck.

Why do some of us have to keep learning these same lessons over and over again? Why do we find this such a difficult danger to overcome? It's because of foolishness in our heart. It's because of careless feet that somehow fail to stay connected with a wise heart.

✤

Wisdom Talking

Proverbs repeatedly points to areas where careless feet return—our choice of words, our friends, the way we spend our time and money. What is a personal story of victory from one of these areas—a time when you changed the direction of careless feet? How do you still struggle with other areas?

Day 3
Quick Fists

A fool's lips lead to strife,
and his mouth provokes a beating.
Proverbs 18:6

Remember the fights we had on the playground when we were kids? Guys and girls would come running from everywhere just to watch, screaming the whole time, going crazy. And when things got really out of hand and threatened to spill over into an after-school brawl, I remember the whispered announcements that spread like wildfire the rest of the day, how these same two guys were scheduled to settle things behind the building at 4:00. *Be there!*

We laugh about it now—all the shoving and punching, the bloody noses, the torn clothing. It's so foolish. So childish. So dumb.

After all, we don't fight anymore, do we?

Well, maybe not the way we fought as kids. But what does it take to set you off? What conditions can come together to cause you to say something ugly, to flare up with a smart remark, to strike a low blow that may be subtle in tone but violent by design?

I've come up with three levels of offense to help you think through this. If you get to level three, you're doing a little better than most.

Level 1: Do you get angry when you're ignored?

If someone is walking down the hallway and doesn't speak to you, does that make you think, "Hey, they saw me standing right there, and they didn't say a word to me." Or maybe, "I did _____ and nobody even said thanks." Are you ready to come out of your chair at somebody when that happens?

Level 2: Do you get angry when you're insulted? You say, "If somebody ignores me, I just ignore them. But if somebody insults me, that's when we're going to have a problem. How dare they say that to me! Don't they know who they're talking to?"

> It is honorable for a man to resolve a dispute, but any fool can get himself into a quarrel.
> PROVERBS 20:3

Level 3: Do you get angry when someone inflicts pain? Do you say, "I can take being ignored. If someone insults me, I just let it roll off my back. But if someone inflicts me, if someone causes me physical, financial, or emotional pain, that's when I find it hardest not to retaliate."

Now, while you're measuring what level of offense it takes before you fight back, take a moment to consider the number one characteristic Jesus displayed in the days leading up to the ordeal of Good Friday.

You remember the scene. They spat on him. They pressed a crown of thorns upon his head. Groups of people came forward to falsely accuse him. They made up things about him. They lied about him. And what did both Herod and Pilate observe above everything else about him? *His silence.* He said nothing. They would look at him and shake their heads, half taunting, half begging, "Aren't you going to say anything?" But Jesus stood silently before them all. He offered not one word of retaliation.

Now let's clarify one thing. Jesus was not silent because he didn't have a defense; Jesus was silent to fulfill prophecy (Isaiah 53:7, Acts 8:32). In 1 Peter 2:23, we get some inside information about what was going on inside Jesus' silent demeanor: "When he was reviled, he did not revile in return; when he suffered, he did not threaten, but continued entrusting himself to him who judges justly." Should we do less?

Quick fists. Sharp comebacks. Sensitive reflexes. These are the marks of a fool, the very things that often keep us from looking like the Lord we claim to serve.

Wisdom Talking

Think of the last time you were insulted, offended, or hurt. How was your response like or unlike Jesus' model?

Day 4
Loose Lips

The proud speech of a fool brings a rod of discipline,
but the lips of the wise protect them.
Proverbs 14:3

The most obvious thing we see in the life of a person characterized by foolishness is not what he does or what he thinks but what he says. The words of a fool are usually among the first things to rat him out.

Foolish people have *loose lips*.

Please hear me now: I'm not saying that there's anything wrong or ungodly about being talkative. Some of us are wired to be more outgoing and engaging than others. James 1:19 does warn us to be "quick to hear" and "slow to speak," but this is not a condemnation of a sanguine personality.

Nor does it mean that fun and games are contrary to Christianity. I think we sometimes forget this. It's not unspiritual to joke around. Having a good sense of humor isn't something we have to use behind God's back. I believe that Jesus Christ loved to laugh, and Proverbs 17:22 calls joyfulness "good medicine."

Loose lips does not describe people who are witty or who make us laugh. There's absolutely nothing sinful about that. May God free us from serious, sober unattractive cheerlessness. What a drag! Of all people on the earth, Christians have every reason to laugh.

But the Lord's wisdom teaches us to be good stewards of our words. We are not to use them as weapons to cause pain or injury. We're not to say things that never should have been said.

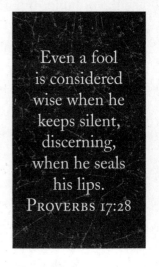

Even a fool is considered wise when he keeps silent, discerning, when he seals his lips.
PROVERBS 17:28

This is one subject that strikes pretty close to home for me. I became very aware as a young man that this was an area where I could easily stumble. I remember well the day, after I had started serving on a church staff, when a godly pastor told me quite bluntly over lunch, "James, you have loose lips." And I was like, "What are you talking about? I can keep a secret."

"That's not what I mean," he said. "I'm just saying when you're under pressure, you sometimes say things that hurt people."

That was hard for me to hear, but I knew he was right. Even today, I'm not a hundred percent beyond this. I still struggle with it from time to time. But it is not foolish to be honest about our struggles; it is only foolish to act like they're no big deal. Only a fool thinks he can afford to live with a few sins, especially the ones that God knows are the hardest ones for us to overcome. Wisdom calls us to deal with our own shortcomings, including *loose lips*.

So God has been growing me in wisdom to heed biblical counsel such as the kind found in Proverbs 10:19—"When there are many words, sin is unavoidable, but the one who controls his lips is wise."

I remember my mom saying from the time I was a little kid, "I am the master of my unspoken words, and the slave to those that should have remained unsaid." There's a lot of wisdom in those words—and there's a lot of foolishness we can keep *out* of our words if we obey what God's wisdom is saying to us.

⊕

Wisdom Talking

Tighten up your loose lips. Put yourself on a diet— limit the number of words you say today. Choose to allow what comes out of your mouth to be based solely on what is healthy and good. (Read Ephesians 4:29.)

Day 5
Roaming Eyes

Wisdom is the focus of the perceptive,
but a fool's eyes roam to the ends of the earth.
Proverbs 17:24

Some people are always looking for something—
something new, something fresh, something that's
long been on their list of wishes but hasn't yet made it
into their portfolio of experiences and possessions.

Another one of the Hebrew words that's used in
the Old Testament to represent foolishness is *nabal*
(pronounced, naw-BAWL). It means someone who
lacks spiritual perception, one who's always looking
for something. He's never sure what it is, but he's
certain that if he had it, he'd be a lot happier. *Nabal* is
the word used in Psalm 14:1, where David declares,
"The fool says in his heart, 'God does not exist.'" This
is the person who rejects the existence of God and
then spends the rest of his life looking for something
else to satisfy the need only God can fill.

Nothing is so far off the fool's path that it can't
draw his gaze, a condition which can give him all
kinds of eye trouble:

Materialistic eyes. This is the person who's driving in traffic, spots a sleek sports car passing him in the express lane, and says, "I think I'd be a whole lot happier if I was driving a car like that." That's foolishness. It's the person at the mall who says, "I'll take this, and that, and one of these, and one of those . . ."

Distracted eyes. I'm sure you've known certain people who never seem to be settled. They are constantly

Let your eyes look forward; fix your gaze straight ahead. Don't turn to the right or to the left.
PROVERBS 4:25, 27

changing gears and setting their sights on something else. "I need a new hobby. I need a new job. I need a new career. I need a new church." They move with no clear purpose, from fad to fad, from meaningless point A to unfulfilling point B. "Let's be leaders in the PTA. No, let's refinish the basement. No, let's join a gym." If you're distracted and restless, I guarantee you that others shake their heads and wonder, "What's he into now? What's her new thing going to be this year?" Distracted eyes are a sure sign that foolishness has crept in.

Lustful eyes. It never ceases to amaze me the way our eyes can be drawn to sin. Why is it we men don't seem to get a clue that women *do* notice when we're not looking at their eyes?

One of my best friends has challenged me in this. Together we work very hard at keeping our eyes pure. When anything comes on the television that is seductive, sensual, or disrespectful of women, we just look away.

You can too. Close your eyes if you need to; focus on something else in the room. Why do I choose to do this? Because I don't have eyes to see women treated in that way, nor do I want to look on any woman other than my wife.

David said in Psalm 101:3, "I will set no wicked thing before mine eyes" (KJV). Men, you've got to know that this honors your wife—and the Lord—in a big way.

May God free us from the foolishness of roaming eyes that are not satisfied with what we have been given, always wanting what our eyes can see.

✠

Wisdom Talking

Materialistic eyes. Distracted eyes. Lustful eyes. Which of these forms of eye trouble are the most prevalent in your life? Say it out loud right now, "Lord, I want to honor you with my eyes. Today, help me change the focus of my _____ (materialistic, distracted, lustful) eyes." Now, acting in faith, draw up a practical plan to guard your eyes.

Day 6
Plugged Ears

A fool's way is right in his own eyes,
but whoever listens to counsel is wise.
Proverbs 12:15

Of all the characteristics of foolishness, the most prominent and troubling one is *plugged ears*—when you're not really listening. All other descriptions of foolishness eventually find themselves under this one.

If you come across a fool—at work, at church, in your neighborhood, in your extended family—don't try to tell him he's headed in the wrong direction with his life unless you're fully prepared to get your head bitten off. A fool is always deeply persuaded that what he's doing is right. He's not going to listen to anybody else about it.

This concept is actually wrapped around the most common Hebrew word for "fool," which appears forty-nine times in the book of Proverbs—*keciyl*—(pronounced, kes-SEEL). These kinds of people are literally "blockheads"—they have a dull and closed mind, and they're too thick-headed to realize it. They are utterly convinced that they know what they're doing, and anyone who disagrees with them is just dead wrong.

Know anybody like that? I'll bet you do. Ever been like that yourself? Some of us have been, for sure.

What makes this so terribly dangerous is that this plugged-ear foolishness is the first thing God must get rid of if he's going to give you a heart of wisdom. Foolishness is so hard to destroy because it's so hard to detect. You can't detect it in your own life, in fact, if your ears are plugged up. So before you can become someone known for godly character and trustworthy advice, your plugged ears need to be scrubbed out.

> The mind of the discerning acquires knowledge, and the ear of the wise seeks it.
> PROVERBS 18:15

As children, when someone was trying to say something to us that we didn't want to hear, remember what we did to shut them out? We'd clap our hands over our ears and talk (or hum or sing) or make nonsense noises like "La-la-la-la-la" loudly enough to drown out their voices. As adults, we've developed our own more sophisticated ways of not listening.

Suppose someone says he'd like to meet for breakfast, and they share with us some things we need to hear about ourselves. We listen carefully. We say "Thank you, I appreciate your input very much." As we get back in our car, we make a mental note never to say *yes* again if he asks to get together. Then we just go on living as we were.

Perhaps someone jots us a note that says, "You know, I love you in the Lord and feel the need to challenge you in this area." We say, "Yes, thank you, I appreciate that so much." But we say to our spouse or another friend, "Can you believe what she said to me?" *Plugged ears.* We're foolish when we don't listen to other people.

Most often when I have heard the voice of God, it has been through someone who cared about me and loved me enough to sit down with me and say, "It goes like this." May God keep our ears from being plugged up when others are talking truth.

Wisdom Talking

What's some of the best advice you ever got? Who did it come from? How did you receive it? What difference has it made in your life? How have you changed because of it?

Day 7
Teachable People

A rebuke cuts into a perceptive person
more than a hundred lashes into a fool.
Proverbs 17:10

Allow me to paraphrase the above verse: *You can get more through to a wise person with one gentle conversation than you can to a fool by whacking him over the head a hundred times.*

Some people won't listen no matter what. You can tell him the same thing over and over again, but you'll get the same response every time. Not so with those whose hearts are being trained by wisdom! If you get in tune with God and his will for your life, you will reap the rewards of being teachable. How do you know when you're being teachable? Here are five good clues:

1. You know you're teachable when people give you input. When you're not teachable, people don't generally risk telling you stuff. Why should they? Imagine their conversations: *"I'm* not gonna tell him; *you* tell him. The last time I tried to tell him, *Chernobyl!* Meltdown for miles!"* If you react abrasively any time someone instructs or corrects you, don't expect to get any input from others. You'll know you're teachable when people tell you things you need to hear. Roll out the red carpet to welcome a good word.

2. You know you're teachable when you see measurable growth and character development. When good changes start happening in your life, you know you're doing something valuable with the information you're getting. You know you're teachable when others' advice produces tangible results in you.

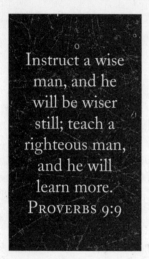

Instruct a wise man, and he will be wiser still; teach a righteous man, and he will learn more.
PROVERBS 9:9

3. You know you're teachable when you don't have to answer back to your critic with a defense. More often than I ever wanted to be, I find myself in situations where I'm giving people input. I don't love it. It's never easy. But I love it when the person who needs to hear a difficult thing about himself or about his situation is open-hearted and just listens. He doesn't have to say, "Now, hold it, you just hang on there a second. You don't understand . . ." I really dread those conversations. But people who are receptive to God's transforming truth are the ones who flourish in life.

4. You know you're teachable when you don't have to return the favor. The classic symptom of an unteachable spirit is after listening to someone's honest, loving counsel, you say, "Fine. Now, let me tell *you* something." You've got an unteachable person on your hands when he can't humbly receive your words and say, "Thank you for telling me."

5. *You know you're teachable when over time you hear something different for a change.* If people have been telling you the same stuff for years but still see the need to remind you about it again, you're not teachable. You should be over that by now and on to the next lesson.

Wisdom is not something we know; it's something we do. Only when we allow God to give us teachable hearts will he show us what we need to know in order to help us change what we do. The biggest fool of all is the person who knows from God what to do and who won't do it. That person is not teachable.

✠

Wisdom Talking

How have you experienced one (or more) of these test statements in the last few weeks? If you read this and didn't once ask yourself, "Am I like that?" you may be in trouble. Take this list of five questions before the Lord and say, "Lord, show me—teach me." Teachability means you're open to changing what he reveals to you.

Day 8
Ticket to Happiness

Happy is a man who finds wisdom
and who acquires understanding.
Proverbs 3:13

When you think of wisdom, what's the first thing that comes to mind? An old man propped up in his rocking chair, dispensing the little truisms he's gathered up from his many years on earth?

For too many of us, wisdom is not a "now" concept. It's an old man thing, a guy who's searched for wisdom over a long, hard quest of life and has finally made it to his destination. He's found wisdom at last.

But wisdom is not just for later. Wisdom is for this very moment. It looks good on people who still have hair, who still can go places, who still have their original knees and hips. The biblical concept of wisdom is not grey hair but sheer vibrancy.

Wisdom keeps you alive and happy.

The Bible teaches that you're young only once, but you can be a fool for life. There is absolutely no correlation between age and wisdom. Some of the most foolish people in the world are people in their seventies and eighties who have never learned anything of lasting value in their long walk on earth—not from God, not from wise family members and friends, not from experience, not from life. But I know people who are as young as ten years old in their walk with Christ, yet who possess such wisdom and counsel and attractiveness in their manner and conversation, it's amazing.

God doesn't wait to pour out his wisdom on those who are too old to do much about it. Instead, he lavishes his wisdom on anyone—young *or* old— who has an open heart willing to listen, who really desires to receive from him, who is hungry to let God teach her from his Word and by his Spirit.

> Anyone who listens to me is happy, watching at my doors every day, waiting by the posts of my doorway.
> PROVERBS 8:34

Do you think wisdom is uncool, that it's sort of a semi-geeky, unplugged, whacked-out, other-worldly kind of pursuit, that it might not go with your outfit or fit in too well at the places you go and the crowd you run with? I'm telling you, that is the opposite of biblical teaching on wisdom.

The wise person is the practical, down-to-earth person who really knows what's going on. They're not sober and stiff and stern and stodgy. The wiser Jesus became (Luke 2:52), the more people wanted to be around him. It'll be the same with you. If you have wisdom, get ready for your phone to ring, because there's not a whole lot of wisdom to go around in this world, and those who are always in the process of receiving it from God are hard to resist.

It's time right now to start seeking after wisdom, to reach after it with all your heart.

You'll be so happy you did.

✛

Wisdom Talking

Is there somebody about your age who seems to have a lot of godly wisdom? How do you think they got it? Proverbs says to "seek wisdom" and to "look for it." How's your hunt going? Where have you found it recently?

Day 9
Work It Out

Go to the ant, you slacker!
Observe its ways and become wise.
Proverbs 6:6

We live in a country that was built through hard work but is increasingly occupied by lazy citizens—people who don't want to work or know how to work.

This is not a new problem. Almost 3,000 years ago when Solomon, the wisest man who ever lived, wrote down his wisdom, much of what he had to say was about work. He wanted to show how essential it is that a strong work ethic be woven into the fabric of who we are. He knew we needed to hear two things very clearly: *work is good* and *laziness is foolishness.*

Is this a concept as current as today's news, or what?! A company can hardly hire the people it wants if it doesn't pipe in the right kind of music, paint the walls the right color, and give them a state-of-the-art work-out facility. Many corporations struggle to limit Internet access as they find their employees secretly wasting hours behind closed doors, surfing the net and having fun but not doing much of anything productive.

Still, anyone looking honestly and objectively at themselves can see that life without work becomes empty and meaningless. Work is not supposed to be the thing we *have* to do so we can do the things we *want* to do. Work is the joy of life—laboring, investing ourselves, spending ourselves.

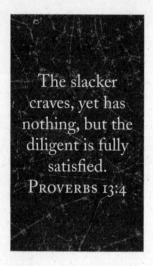

The slacker craves, yet has nothing, but the diligent is fully satisfied.

PROVERBS 13:4

Someone may say, "Wait a minute, I thought God cursed work." You've been reading the book of Genesis, haven't you? Well, read again the first part. Because while God did curse work in Genesis 3 after the Fall, he first said to Adam and Eve, "Be fruitful, multiply, fill the earth, and subdue it. Rule the fish of the sea, the birds of the sky, and every creature that crawls on the earth" (Gen. 1:28). The familiar Bible term for this is "dominion." When God finished giving these work instructions to Adam and Eve, he declared all his pronouncements and activities of that day "very good" (Gen. 1:31).

Yes, after sin entered the human experience, God stepped forward and declared a judgment on work (Gen. 3:17–19), saying in effect, "From now on, this good thing that I created called 'work' is going to take sweat to make happen." But listen: just because God said that work would be *hard* doesn't mean he said work would no longer be *good*. All through Scripture, the value of work is championed and applauded.

"The thief must no longer steal. Instead, he must do honest work with his own hands" (Eph. 4:28). "The laborer is worthy of his wages" (1 Tim. 5:18). Paul went so far as to say, "If anyone isn't willing to work, he should not eat" (2 Thess. 3:10). And in one of the clearest verses of all, he said, "Whatever you do, do it enthusiastically, as something done for the Lord and not for men" (Col. 3:23).

Work is part of God's original design. It's not a waste of your time to clean the basement or return phone calls or assemble products on an assembly line or write a term paper or rake leaves. Work is good!

✠

Wisdom Talking

If your boss could fill out an anonymous survey right now on your work habits, how would you rate on a scale of 1 to 10?
- Will do what is needed to get the job done.
- Will work smart and hard.
- Will consistently go above and beyond the call.
- What other questions about your job applies?

Day 10
Lazy Habits

Without leader, administrator, or ruler,
[the ant] prepares its provisions in summer.
Proverbs 6:7–8

What a reproach that mankind, fashioned in the image of Almighty God, should have to learn from the lowest of all insects. Yet as Solomon made his way down the animal chain, he had to go all the way from human beings to ants to find a good example of what work is all about.

When I was a kid, we used to step on ants for fun. Now I find out they're supposed to be my teacher. It's embarrassing.

But, ants have some lessons to teach about work and the dangers of laziness:

1. Lazy people require constant supervision. At the house where I grew up, the driveway was made of concrete, and there were all these little cracks where the ants would build their anthills. I can remember just sitting down on blisteringly hot, summer days and watching them (sometimes with a magnifying glass!) marveling at how hard they worked.

Yet they don't seem to have a boss or a significant authority structure. They just all have a job to do, and apparently they do it.

How come we humans can't seem to work hard like that when the boss is out of town, when there's no one who knows what we're doing except God and us? Lazy people won't do much without being watched.

2. Laziness tends to produce inconsistent effort. A lazy person is usually a here-and-there, off-and-on worker, rarely if ever pushing himself to do more or work harder. I'm not endorsing workaholism here. I'm not saying that the opposite of laziness is non-stop work. The biblical message is not to work long hours but to work *hard,* to put in a full effort for a reasonable amount of time.

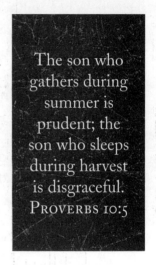

The son who gathers during summer is prudent; the son who sleeps during harvest is disgraceful.
PROVERBS 10:5

You say, "That's what we're arguing about all the time at our house. How much is reasonable?" The Bible points out two purposes of work: a) *to provide*— "If anyone does not provide for his own relatives, and especially for his own household, he has denied the faith and is worse than an unbeliever" (1 Tim. 5:8) and b) *to avoid poverty.* We should try to stay balanced perfectly between these two, neither overdoing it or underdoing it. Proverbs 30:8–9 says: "Give me neither poverty nor wealth; feed me with the food I need.

Otherwise, I might have too much and deny You, saying, 'Who is the Lord?' or I might have nothing and steal, profaning the name of my God." What a beautiful picture of the balance he desires in our work. God calls us only to steady, consistent effort.

3) Laziness only leads to more fatigue. Proverbs 6:9 says it this way: "How long will you stay in bed, you slacker? When will you get up from your sleep?" Lazy people, it seems, are always needing to rest, even though they haven't done anything to get tired from.

If you had a good home, you probably grew up hearing these words a lot: "Idle hands are the devil's workshop." That's a great truth to remember. When there's nothing to do, this often ends up being a bad thing. Laziness breeds more laziness and creates an aversion to work—a disdain for one of God's greatest callings on our lives.

So go check out the ants. Watch for people who are doing this right. Look and learn.

Wisdom Talking

How does your boss's presence influence your productivity? Conduct an experiment today—work like the only one watching you is the Lord.

Day 11
Sudden Death

A little sleep, a little slumber . . .
and poverty will come like a robber.
Proverbs 6:10–11

The dangers that come along with laziness, as seen in the book of Proverbs, are not just incidental damage. It's not the sour grapes of hard workers wishing they could be as carefree and casual as lazy people are. No, there are some serious side-effects of habitual inactivity, and the Bible is very direct about pointing them out.

There's this one, for example: *sudden poverty.*

You may think things are going along pretty well. Nobody seems to be noticing that you're slacking off, taking long lunches, leaving early, wasting time. You think you're getting away with it. No big deal.

Or maybe it's laziness in an area outside of your job. Maybe you're being lax about your spending habits, or your moral alertness, or your church attendance.

Then . . . BOOM!

That's when consequences sneak up and attack, like an armed man holding you at gunpoint. You flinch and resist, but there's no getting out of this one. You're caught with no means of reversal. Poverty has dropped down on you unaware, and getting your life back is going to take a lot more work than you ever wanted to put in.

Poverty in the Scripture is not always talking about *financial* poverty. The bigger issue is always the spiritual element, the part that refers to poverty of the soul. When Solomon said, "The slacker craves yet has nothing, but the diligent is fully satisfied" (Prov. 13:4), he was talking about more than just having a nice roof over your head and food in the fridge. He was saying that hard work produces something good in *your soul!* Likewise, laziness produces something awful and debilitating in the heart of the slothful person.

Don't love sleep, or you will become poor; open your eyes, and you'll have enough to eat.
PROVERBS 20:13

I remember as a kid being taught to work. One of the greatest contributions my mother has made in my life is her work ethic. Her maiden name is Sherwood. Because she liked her maiden name so much and was so proud of the work ethic in her family, she gave me her maiden name as my middle name—Sherwood.

Growing up, I always thought that was such a hassle. I didn't really like my middle name very much. But you know, I don't feel that way anymore. I remember when I worked with my dad even as a six or seven-year-old, I'd come into the house tired, and my mom would get me a drink and put her arm around me and say, "You're a Sherwood. Sherwoods know how to work." She'd give me a hug and pull me up in her lap, and say, "You're such a good worker, son, just like your grandfather," who worked on a construction site into his mid-seventies.

My mother was pouring into my heart the fact that work is a good thing. To come to the end of the day, to arrive home exhausted and tired, and to sit down at the table and say, "I worked hard today," is something to be proud of and feel good about.

There is a sense of relief and accomplishment, a settled contentment in the soul of a man, that can never be attained by goofing off and watching television. The destiny of the lazy is only pain, regret, and poverty. It won't wait long to show up.

✠

Wisdom Talking

Who has positively influenced your attitude about work? What has been the fruit from their lives? If it's possible, write or call to thank them for instilling this godly characteristic into your life.

Day 12
Nowhere Fast

A door turns on its hinge,
and a slacker, on his bed.
Proverbs 26:14

Think about the front or the back door of your house, the one that gets the most traffic as you and your family and guests enter and exit. Ever wonder how many times that door has swung open and shut over the years?

But guess what? *It hasn't gone anywhere.*

It may have moved back and forth a thousand times, but when you push it closed at the end of the day, it's right where it was this morning.

That's kind of what a lazy person is like. He turns on his bed, but he doesn't go anywhere. He doesn't accomplish anything. He doesn't change or improve or pick up yardage. He doesn't make any forward progress. Because laziness has overcome him, because he's lost his desire to override his own selfish appetites, he just swims the same course every day. Never making up ground. Never putting himself in a better position. Never getting anywhere.

As a pastor, I have the opportunity to look into the eyes of more human weakness than just about anybody else does. My work puts me in a position to encounter people dealing with all kinds of problems. I don't know of any human problem that is harder to see changed than the lack of a real work ethic.

I've seen God change all kinds of things in people. I've seen him correct amazing shortages of character and other deficiencies that we all have. But I honestly can't think of anything harder to change in a person than the lack of a vibrant work ethic.

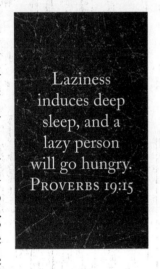

Laziness induces deep sleep, and a lazy person will go hungry.
PROVERBS 19:15

Early in my ministry, I had the misfortune of working with a lazy pastor. He'd come in to work at 10:00 in the morning and go home at 3:00 in the afternoon, with multiple coffee breaks and a lunchtime in between. There I was, a 21-year-old staff member, feeling so ashamed when people would come to me and ask, "What's going on? Where is he?" I didn't know what to say. I didn't know what to do. I just remember feeling very disillusioned, promising myself that if I was ever in the position of leading a church, it would not be that way.

I remember years ago when we started the church where I serve now, we promised that our staff was going to work as hard as any man or woman in the church. I can tell you that when a staff member doesn't like this arrangement, that person doesn't work with us very long.

You may say, "That sounds really harsh." No, I'll tell you what sounds really harsh to me: it's when people who are out there laboring in the marketplace bring their tithes to church week after week, and put them in the offering plate by faith, trusting God to use their investment for eternal results, and then they find out that the people who have the privilege of working for God's kingdom don't even work as hard as they do—that's not right.

If you have a problem with your work ethic, I'm warning you about something you probably already know: *you're going to have a really hard time changing*. But don't give up. God can lead you out of this if you're honest about your struggle and dedicated to letting him help you. It's work, but it's worth it.

❖

Wisdom Talking

Has anyone ever called you lazy? Were they right? What areas of your life would be improved by more effort and perseverance?

Day 13
Who Cares?

The slacker buries his hand in the bowl;
he is too weary to bring it to his mouth.
Proverbs 26:15

This is one thing I just hate about laziness: the way it produces this feeling of, "I don't care. It doesn't matter. It's not that important." If you've ever been at a place in your life where you haven't been exerting yourself for several days, weeks, or months on end, you know how it inevitably leads to this conclusion about life, about your relationships, about your responsibilities, about everything:

"Who cares?"

Do you want to be someone who's fired up about living? Someone who wakes up at 6:30 in the morning and can't wait for the day to begin? Someone who's lying there itching for the alarm to go off, already clicking off in your head the steps you plan to employ to take full advantage of today? Someone who's excited to see what the next opportunity may hold if you throw your full weight into it? Someone who loves the invigorating smell of a new challenge?

Then open your eyes to the role that laziness may be playing in dragging down your attitudes and passions, leaving you feeling blah and unmotivated. Understand that your zealousness to "escape" may be the very thing that is sapping your energy, much more so than the effort you're expending at work.

It's true—*laziness can wear you out!*

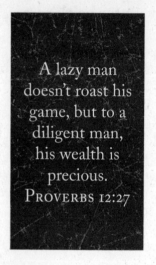

A lazy man doesn't roast his game, but to a diligent man, his wealth is precious.

PROVERBS 12:27

In fact, I don't know of a quicker path to depression than the one paved by lazy attitudes and work habits. I've seen a lot of people who've been given fat pensions or some other escape from work who have just dried up and become miserable.

That's because along the way, they started seeing work as an awful thing they *had* to do rather than a wonderful thing they had the *privilege* of doing. There's something about spending yourself in hard work that produces energy and passion in your heart and soul, just as there's something about laziness that produces apathy and makes you think, *"Who cares?"*

It doesn't have to be this way. God didn't create you to run from reality but to transform it. He made you with an empty spot that can only be filled by accomplishment and service. Ephesians 2:10 says we have been "created in Christ Jesus for good works," made to bear the image of a hard-working God.

It's so easy to grow soft and forget this. It's very natural for us to live for the weekend and avoid work at all possible costs. It's also very easy to lose the will to care about God and other people when life gets hard and the burdens of the day seem too heavy to bear.

It isn't easy to spot this tendency in yourself. I've had the awful task of having to face people directly who have a significant problem with their work ethic, people who aren't providing for their family. Other people have joined me in trying to challenge them, lovingly and fervently pleading with them to see what's going on. Yet I've seen them walk out and reject the message. I've heard them say, "You're *all* crazy! I don't have a problem!" It's tragic.

Stay open to the influence of others and God's Word. Let them lead you to a place of purpose—a place that makes "who cares" a thing of the past.

Wisdom Talking

If you want to be wise, catch yourself from thinking or saying, "Who cares" or "What does it matter?" Instead consider why you momentarily want to shut down. Pray immediately that God would keep your heart and head in the game.

Day 14
Christian Work

Won't He who protects your life know?
Won't He repay a person according to his work?
Proverbs 24:12

I want to leave these readings on work and laziness with a final challenge for you to be stellar in your performance, especially if you are the only one in your workplace (or one of a few) who knows the Lord Jesus Christ as your Savior. The testimony of a strong work ethic goes a long way to validate the claims of your faith. If being a follower of Christ has left enough of a mark on you to affect the way you deal with employees, or handle conflict, or stay at the job until closing time, others will notice.

You may say, "I don't have the gifts and abilities some people have." Maybe, but you can still put out the effort. Thomas Edison, famous for inventing many of the phenomenal things we enjoy today, said these now-familiar words: "Genius is 1% inspiration and 99% perspiration." Think about that as you adopt the following principles from God's Word for your daily marching orders.

1) I work for honesty before profit. Proverbs 11:1 is a striking picture of God observing the marketplace: "Dishonest scales are detestable to the Lord, but an accurate weight is His delight." When farmers used to bring their grain to market, they would place their crops on one side of the scale. Then a number of measured weights would be placed on the other side to determine exactly how much was being sold. But dishonest weights—the thumb on the scale to tip things in your favor—God comes right out and says he hates.

Every time you make a deal, sell a product, or conduct a business transaction, if you do it fairly and justly, it honors God. What an excellent exchange— your honest work for God's blessing and delight.

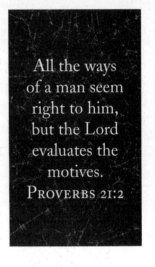

All the ways of a man seem right to him, but the Lord evaluates the motives.
PROVERBS 21:2

2) I work for provision before pleasure. Proverbs 24:27 says: "Complete your outdoor work, and prepare your field; afterwards, build your house." In other words, your work is not only about harvesting benefits for yourself.

The farmer who plants a few crops to sell, then channels all his resources into building a beautiful home for himself is not wise. He's putting pleasure before provision. But the wise person isn't skimming every inch off his profits to increase his lifestyle. He's working to provide. Plain and simple. He's taking out of his gross income only the amount required to provide for his family's needs, not scavenging his revenues to spend every single increase.

3) I work for God before people. If you're a housewife, you're not working for your husband; you're working for God. If you're employed in the marketplace, you're not working for the boss, the foreman, the president, or the shareholders; you're working for God. He's the one you'll give an account to. He's the one you need to stay focused upon.

Honesty before profit. Provision before pleasure. God before people. These are the biblical principles that will keep your work satisfying and productive—and your heart at rest in his will for your life.

⊕

Wisdom Talking

Ask yourself: Does my employer, my family, my customer benefit from my work, or are they victimized by my desire for profit? Am I wise to invest my gains for long-term benefit? How does my attitude need to adjust considering that I work primarily for God's pleasure?

Day 15
Richer than Ever

For wisdom is better than precious stones,
and nothing desirable can compare with it.
Proverbs 8:11

Have you ever been to a museum and seen the crown jewels or an exhibit of rare and valuable art?

Have you ever stared into a candy shop window and drooled over and craved the chocolate slices sitting on wax paper behind the glass?

Have you ever sat at a sporting event or a musical performance, and wished you had the talent to hit a major-league fastball, play a clarinet in the symphony, or sing to the adoration of applauding fans?

Closer to home, have you ever been waiting for Christmas, assured that at least a few of the presents under the tree were for you, and let yourself hope they contained the one thing—the one big thing—you've been wishing someone would give you this year?

We all have dreams and wishes. Some things we've wanted our entire lives: certain goals we've wanted to achieve, certain milestones we've wanted to cross, certain possessions we've hoped to acquire. The book of Proverbs tells us truthfully that of all the things we could possibly want or hope for or desire, nothing compares with wisdom.

Nothing.

Suppose I held out both hands to you. In the fingers of one hand was a crisp $100 bill; in the other hand I held a piece of wisdom. I invited you, "Take one, whichever one you want. In this hand I've got everything you can buy with a hundred dollars, and in my other hand I've got something so tried-and-true that every time you come to a particular choice in life, this piece of wisdom will help you make the right decision, and phenomenal things will happen to you as a result. Which one do you want?"

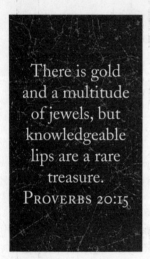

There is gold and a multitude of jewels, but knowledgeable lips are a rare treasure.

PROVERBS 20:15

The Bible says that if God is beginning to place any wisdom in your heart at all, you wouldn't have to think twice. Rather than being baited by a $100 bill, you would disdain the temporary pleasure of earthly possessions for the unrivaled value of God's heart and mind and understanding. In fact, you would embrace it quickly, as though if you didn't act now, it might be lost to you forever. You couldn't bear the thought of going through life without that piece of wisdom.

Wisdom is better than rubies, than precious stones, than all the money in the world. It's better than 4,000 square-foot houses with three-car garages, better than high-def televisions, better than a new dress coat, a college scholarship, or a four-wheel drive. Of all the things you could want or desire, nothing is worthy of being compared to the possibility of having real wisdom.

Daniel 12:3 says, "Those who are wise will shine like the bright expanse of the heavens, and those who lead many to righteousness, like the stars forever and ever." Whatever you have, if you have wisdom, it is the most valuable line-item in your asset column.

If you want something that's really special, wisdom is always the best thing going.

✣

Wisdom Talking

Put in your own words why you think wisdom is to be desired more than gold—more than possessions—more than anything. Write your statement on the first page of your checkbook.

Day 16
Fool's Gold

> Such are the paths of all who pursue gain dishonestly;
> it takes the lives of those who profit from it.
> Proverbs 1:19

Treat it foolishly, and money will take you down.

Some people may think that's too dramatic of a statement. "Are you saying that money actually has the capacity to destroy a person's life?"

No, that's not what *I'm* saying. That's what *God's Word* is saying.

Money has the power to reach into people's lives, to come down their street, to invade their house, to absolutely devastate all their hopes and dreams for the future, and cast their very soul into hell.

I don't know how many names I'd have to call out before we'd get the message. Here's one: the June 14, 1968, issue of *Life* magazine featured the picture of a young David Kennedy, sitting outside the White House. The picture had been taken several years earlier, and it was inscribed with these words from his uncle: "A future president inspects his property." Signed, John F. Kennedy. But although young David

Kennedy had wealth and status and all the things money could buy, he was found dead by his own hand in 1984 at the age of 28. All the money in the world led only to despair and desperation.

Here's another. See if you can figure out who said these words: "I sit in my house in Buffalo, and sometimes I get so lonely, it's unbelievable. Life has been so good to me. I've got a great wife, good kids, lots of money, my own health, but I'm lonely and bored. I've often wondered why so many rich people commit suicide. Money sure isn't a cure-all." That quote is taken from *People* magazine, 1978, spoken by O. J. Simpson.

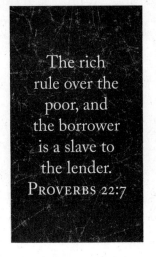

The rich rule over the poor, and the borrower is a slave to the lender.
PROVERBS 22:7

Can money destroy?

Oh yeah.

There used to be two kinds of people in our society: the *haves* and the *have-nots*. Now there's a third category that's the largest of all: the *have-not-paid-for-what-they-haves*.

This is far more tragic than we realize. It's much more than an issue of outspending our income.

By far, the number one cause of marital breakdown is money. I'm not talking about deadbeats who are lost without Christ and act the part. The main reason why families come into our churches looking for marital counseling is because of money. They're out of control. They can't handle it. The arguments and the financial pressure are killing them.

Of course, that often leads to divorce. The biggest tragedy of divorce, we know, is the effect it has on our children. Divorce is the number one cause for behavioral disorders in kids. Behavioral disorders are the number one cause of crime—serious crime: armed robbery, rape, and murder.

"Why do we have so much crime in our society?" we ask. Figure it out. People are hurting and confused, and they strike out against others because of the devastation that's happened to them in the home. Back the whole thing up, and it often points to money as being the root source that started it all.

Be careful out there, my friend. Money can kill.

Wisdom Talking

How has your view of money changed over the years as you see how people are changed by it? How have you been changed by having a lot or perhaps just a little of it?

Day 17
Money Trouble

The house of the righteous has great wealth,
but trouble accompanies the income of the wicked.
Proverbs 15:6

Money can cause us trouble. Big trouble. If you're making money but you're not completely sold out to a godly, biblical purpose for using it, then the verse above calls you a troubling name—"wicked." You may be saved, you may be one of God's people, but this doesn't keep you from finding yourself in the category of the "wicked" as far as your behavior with money is concerned.

Sound serious? It is. We need to know what we're dealing with here. This money business has eternal consequences.

Proverbs 9 gives us a taste of this. The context of this passage is a foolish, clamorous woman who's talking to a simple-minded man. She calls him in off the road and says to him (verse 17), "Stolen water is sweet, and bread eaten secretly is tasty!" Is she telling the truth to this guy? Is stolen water sweet? Does a soda go down nice and cold even if you rip it off from the store? Does a hot yeast roll taste good even if you snag it before suppertime with no one around to notice? Yes, for a minute. We get a momentary pleasure from things we sneak behind others' backs, things we do purely for our own enjoyment.

But there's also verse 18, which reveals the fact that the person who operates this way on a regular basis "doesn't know that the departed spirits are there." When we use our money only to scratch our itches, thinking we're set for life because of the things it can buy us, *death is there.* Verse 18 goes on to say, "Her guests are in the depths of Sheol [or hell]." The people who live by this mentality find themselves in a pit of death and destruction.

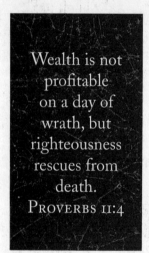

Wealth is not profitable on a day of wrath, but righteousness rescues from death.

PROVERBS 11:4

Never forget: money has a lot more in common with death than with life. It has magnets that tilt a lot harder toward hell than heaven.

Jesus said the same thing another way: "It is easier for a camel to go through the eye of a needle than for a rich person to enter the kingdom of God" (Matt. 19:24). Was he saying it's impossible for a rich person to go to heaven? No. But it's impossible for anyone to get to heaven who isn't fully dependent on Jesus. And doing that on a comfortable six-digit income doesn't come very naturally.

If you could ask some of the people who are suffering in hell this very minute, "How did you get here?" what would they say? Here's guessing that a whole lot of them would say that money was the anchor that pulled them down.

Proverbs 11:4 says, "Wealth is not profitable on a day of wrath, but righteousness rescues from death." When we appear before God's judgment seat, a lot of people who thought their money could buy them everything they wanted will find out their ATM cards have unexpectedly expired. Fishing in their pockets for anything they can use for I.D., they'll discover that only "righteousness"—the righteousness of Christ—will do them any good.

So even if you have lots of money today, let Christ's righteousness be all you're truly counting on. Where money can often lead us into trouble, Jesus will always lead us toward home.

✤

Wisdom Talking

Be honest about the hold that money has on you. How much of your time is invested in thinking about it, worrying about it, making plans for it? What promise do you think money is making to you?

Day 18
Honest Gain

Wealth obtained by fraud will dwindle,
but whoever earns it through labor will multiply it.
Proverbs 13:11

Most of us would never deceive our business partners. We wouldn't lie and cheat on our taxes. We wouldn't steal from the company and try to cover it up with shady accounting practices.

But a lot of us live a lie. We tell people what our priorities are—the noble things, the godly things—but we neglect God's priorities in the way we earn our money. This, too, is dishonesty, and the book of Proverbs warns us to run away from it.

Perhaps you face dilemmas like these in your workplace: You can be honest and lose your job, or you can be dishonest and keep it. You can be honest and lose the deal, or you can be dishonest and swing it. You can be honest and give reliable counsel, or you can be dishonest and tell them what they want to hear. The temptations that swirl around these choices are strong, and the struggle is real. If you are not gaining your income honestly, if you are compromising your integrity, if you are planting seeds of willful (though seemingly excusable) disobedience, *it will destroy you.*

You also run the risk of destroying those who follow after you. Proverbs 20:7 says: "The one who lives with integrity is righteous; his children who come after him will be happy." Many of us feel pressure to give stuff to our kids. That's one reason why we run the risk of earning it dishonestly. We want to give them a leg up, give them nicer things than we ever had, give them a better chance, send them to a better college. While we're spending ourselves like mad to do it, we are ripping from their grasp the things they desperately need: a loving family, a good example, a strong spiritual foundation.

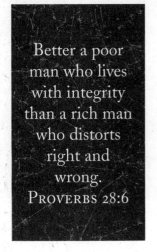

Better a poor man who lives with integrity than a rich man who distorts right and wrong.
PROVERBS 28:6

You say, "I'm going to give them both—a life with Christ and a lot of other stuff, too." I wish Jesus had given us some teaching on that, don't you? Or wait, maybe he did: "No one can be a slave of two masters, since either he will hate one and love the other, or be devoted to one and despise the other. You cannot be slaves of God and of money" (Matt. 6:24).

I don't know how many times I've sat in a room with kids, college students, and young adults who were weeping—resentful and angry at parents who had given them *everything* but had withheld themselves. If you think somehow you're helping your kids by giving and giving to them, laboring beyond measure to provide all these things yet denying them *you*, you're wrong.

We would be far better off if we just said to our kids, "No summer camp, no Disney World, no big-ticket Christmas presents, no Ivy League college. Instead, we're going to spend ourselves on you. We're going to pour ourselves into your life. We're going to live with integrity and honesty before you. The things of Christ are not just going to be *verbalized* in our home; they're going to be lived out. It won't just be the right speech; it'll be the real life, the real thing."

Your kids will thank you for that. They'll say, "My mom, my dad—they're the wisest people I know."

Wealth that is gained dishonestly is destined to be frittered away. When we work hard and honorably for the money we earn, God brings down with it the wisdom we need to manage it.

Wisdom Talking

In what ways do your children's opinions of money (how to spend, earn, and save) need to be corrected?

Day 19
Accurate Estimations

A rich man's wealth is his fortified city;
in his imagination it is a like a high wall.
Proverbs 18:11

People who have wealth tend to think of their money as a strongly held city. It's their protection and security. When they look to the future, they say, "I don't know what's going to happen, but I know we'll be okay because we're converting all our stocks to cash. We'll have a lot of money in the bank."

Hmm. Now, as believers in Jesus Christ, what is supposed to be our strong tower? Who is supposed to be our sole source of acceptance and provision? When we have riches, we naturally look to them instead, expecting them to do for us what only God can do. We really need to keep our money in perspective. Here's a good reason why: "As soon as your eyes fly to it, it disappears, for it makes wings for itself and flies like an eagle to the sky" (Prov. 23:5).

So what follows are five wrong myths about money that we would all do well to understand and work around.

Myth #1) Money will make me happy. Let's not even waste time debating that. Winning this argument is like taking candy from a baby. Many sad stories from history and the Bible, as well as many of our own experiences, prove that money will let us down and leave us unsatisfied. Will money make you happy? Probably just the opposite.

Don't wear yourself out to get rich; stop giving your attention to it.
PROVERBS 23:4

Myth #2) Money will make me content. "If I just had *that*, everything would be great." When we get settled into that new house, when we get this one thing accomplished, when we can get around this corner, when we can finally accumulate enough money in savings to put a down payment on it, then we're going to have everything just like we want it. "All I need is *that!*"—whatever *that* is.

How many times have we said stuff like this? How many times have we discovered that the thing we wanted so badly really *wasn't* all that! Have you ever worked like crazy to try chipping down your credit card bill, and when you finally get it all paid off, what's the first thing you do—go buy something else? You build a mountain of debt all over again. If that isn't bondage to the false notion that money will make us content, I don't know what is. Money can't do that for us.

Myth #3) Money will give me family appreciation. Even if we fail at everything else, we think someday our kids are going to come to us and say, "Dad, you were a really good provider. You were able to afford to give me everything I needed and wanted, and I'll be forever grateful for it." Don't hold your breath. More likely what will happen is, "Dad, you were working so much, you didn't give me yourself. You bought me all this stuff, but all I needed was you."

Myth #4) Money will make me feel better about myself. We think if we just had money, we could hold our heads up higher. We'd look forward to going home for Thanksgiving and having people tell us how successful we are. It's false flattery.

Myth #5) Money will give me acceptance with others. Let me spare you the pain on that one. Proverbs 28:22 says, "A greedy man is in a hurry for wealth; he doesn't know that poverty will come to him." The trouble with money is that it promises big but delivers little.

✠

Wisdom Talking

Have you ever felt tricked by any of the money myths listed above? Share your story with someone younger than you: "Here's what I've learned . . ."

Day 20
Generous Portions

Honor the Lord with your possessions
and with the first produce of your entire harvest.
Proverbs 3:9

My last word on money is probably the first one
we need to remember: *share it generously.* Hold your
income with a loose, open hand. Don't hoard it for
yourself but give it to others, and God will bless you
in return.

Solomon's follow-up to the above verse makes
God's promise clear. When we are faithful to Proverbs
3:9, we reap the reward of Proverbs 3:10—"Then
your barns will be completely filled, and your vats will
overflow with new wine."

If you've been around the church very long, you've
heard this preached and taught a hundred times, but
don't let familiarity take the shine off this concept.
How phenomenal is it that the God of glory chooses
to bless us in response to our giving. He tells us to
give him our "first produce" off-the-top, the first part
of our paycheck before we put it in the bank, before
we do anything else with it. In biblical times, these

"firstfruits" were the first apples off the tree, the first corn that grew on the stalks, the first crops that were harvested from the field. God has gone on record as saying that if we are generous in sharing what he has given, he will give back to us and bless us.

One of the passages God has used to free so many people from their bondage to money and material things is Malachi 3:10—"Bring the full 10 percent into the storehouse so that there may be food in my house. Test me in this way, says the Lord of Hosts. See if I will not open the floodgates of heaven and pour out a blessing for you without measure."

A generous person will be blessed, for he shares his food with the poor.
PROVERBS 22:9

You may say, "Tithing's not for today," but what you really mean is, "I have so many things I need to do (or want to do) with my money, I have a hard time giving. There never seems to be enough to go around."

Five hundred years before the law was given, Abraham brought tithes to Melchizadek. Tithing is not an Old Testament law issue. It is a biblical issue, an outright expectation. Even if it wasn't, should living in an age of grace make us want to do *less* than was required by the law, or more? We should give tithes and beyond, bringing them into the "storehouse," the local church, your place of worship.

Look what God says in return: "Try me. Come on, let's go for it—right here, right now. You do what I've called you to do, and see if I don't do what I've promised. See if I won't bless you in return, even more than you expect." It's almost inconceivable that we should pass up a promise like that, and yet many thousands of us do it on a daily, weekly basis. We hold back and we miss out.

God is looking for people he can trust, people who are ready to go on a faith-building journey with him, an experience that comes complete with a guaranteed return of blessing. I'm not talking about him putting money back in your checking account. I'm talking about the blessing of being on mission with God, allowing him to use your life for his eternal purposes, being able to stay open to his plan for your life, and growing in intimacy with your Creator and Savior.

✢

Wisdom Talking

Go back and read the verses from Malachi again. God is offering you the chance to test him. Has he ever failed you before? Do you know of a special need at your church or someone in ministry or in need that you can bless? Give beyond your comfort zone and trust God to supply your needs.

Day 21
High Impact

The lips of the righteous feed many,
but fools die for lack of sense.
Proverbs 10:21

How long does it take to prepare a holiday meal? I'm talking about those traditional times of Thanksgiving, Christmas, and Easter when the family descends on one house, around one table, with one common goal—stuffing ourselves silly! If you counted up all the time spent in planning, shopping, buying, cooking, and cleaning up after one of these monster meals, most moms and grandmoms would tell you it takes between ten and fifteen hours.

Wow.

But you know what? Even with all the organization and effort that goes into pulling one of those meals off, they often begin with little or no thought to the words that will be shared around the table. After all, what's really more important—that we gorge ourselves on Grandma's mashed potatoes or pumpkin pie, or that we speak and receive the wisdom we need to share at special gatherings like these?

"The lips of the righteous," Solomon said, "feed many." Their words contain a weight and power unlike those of most people. Their influence is not contained to random, infrequent occurrences; rather, their words have a way of multiplying exponentially, too good not to be passed along and repeated. Their words are a regular feast of truth and blessing.

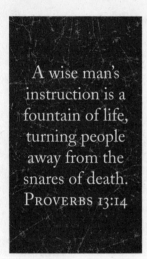

A wise man's instruction is a fountain of life, turning people away from the snares of death.

Proverbs 13:14

I remember going out to my Grandma's as a kid for special holiday dinners. She was one of those people who wanted everybody to sit around one dinner table, no matter how many folks were there. I can remember when my aunts, who are much younger than my dad, would bring their boyfriends, and then their husbands, and then their kids to the table, and it would curve into the living room and extend down the hallway. If you stood at one end and leaned over far enough, you could come close to seeing the other end.

That's the way Grandma wanted it.

I went to so many of those meals, I can't remember them all. The food was always indescribably good, but that's not what I recall the most about it. Instead, I remember my grandmother standing at the head of the table, with everyone ready to eat. Then it would get very quiet. She would begin to share for two or three minutes from her heart, and then she would pray.

I'm talking, pray! She would bow her head and begin to lay hold of God for us, crying out to him for our family to follow him and stay close to him. She would call down his blessing for everyone in the room. Within a matter of forty-five seconds or so, her tears would begin flowing. By the time she said, "In Jesus' name I pray, amen," you were just about ready to go home, because the major thing had already happened. Grandma had prayed, and it was powerful just to hear it.

We all have certain gifts and abilities that allow us to do some things well. Whether it's cooking or sewing or shooting a rifle or delivering a sermon, none of these will ever have any lasting, great impact until it's infused with God's wisdom. When it is, we have the potential to make a huge impact on those around us. That's what wisdom can do.

Wisdom Talking

What kinds of things have you tried to do in order to have a greater impact on others? Which ones have failed, and which ones have succeeded?

Day 22
Good Friends

A righteous man is careful in dealing with his neighbor,
but the ways of wicked men lead them astray.
Proverbs 12:26

For some reason (and I'm not sure why), friendship has fallen on hard times lately. It's not that popular any more.

Romance, on the other hand, has become big-time. Love relationships, sexual relationships, male-female relationships—romance is everywhere. It's in every song, every book, every movie. In fact, I'm afraid we've devalued friendship to the point that, if someone possesses a lot of really good friends but no romantic relationship, that person is thought to be (or thinks himself to be) significantly lacking.

Not so!

Friendship is a priceless gift from God, a choice treasure from his gracious, all-loving hand. I define friendship as "a unique, same-sex relationship where common interests form a bond which stretches and satisfies both people." We are blessed indeed when God brings a friend like that into our life.

But we must be careful about this, because not everyone is good friendship material. Like the old saying Paul quoted in 1 Corinthians 15:33 says, "Bad company corrupts good morals." Friendship will affect your future for good or for bad.

I remember the first day I went to high school. We had about 1,500 students at the school I attended, and I can still remember walking into that building and being blown away by the number of people there—and the many options for making friends.

Don't make friends with an angry man, and don't be a companion of a hot-tempered man.
PROVERBS 22:24

I saw students who seemed to be from the music department, who seemed sort of isolated, off by themselves. There were also the brainiacs. I knew right off the bat, I would never fit into that group. I saw the jocks, the athletes, just walking down the hallway, acting like they had it all together. Maybe they'd be good friends; maybe they wouldn't. I saw the computer geeks, who seemed pretty uncool to my young eyes. (This was long before Bill Gates made his billions and changed the perception.) I saw the druggies, who hung out behind the cafeteria, acting like they were having fun but actually striking out against some internal pain.

Here's the point: after all these years since then, when I think of the people I remember from high school, the ones I've kept up with or heard about, the similarities are amazing. They've almost all tracked in the direction of the group or groups they chose to associate with in high school. They became like the people they hung around with.

We just do.

So whether you're a new high school freshman or an empty-nester in your late fifties—wherever you are in life, young or old—choose your friends wisely. Don't just let work association or next-door neighbor proximity dictate who you spend the bulk of your time with. Don't let a chance meeting, or family ties, or even the church you go to choose your friends for you. Make some deliberate choices; think it through. Decide the kind of people you need to associate with, the ones you intend to call your real, heartfelt, lots-of-time-together friends. Then choose them.

✠

Wisdom Talking

How have you seen this friendship principle bear fruit in your own life? Which friends ended up costing you? Which friends are still blessing your life? List their names. Record tangible ways they have blessed you by their friendship.

Day 23
All-Time Love

A friend loves at all times,
and a brother is born for a difficult time.
Proverbs 17:17

In the verse that directly precedes the well-known thirteenth chapter of 1 Corinthians, Paul set up the awesome, articulate words that follow by saying, "I will show you an even better way." Or as we are more used to hearing it, "a more excellent way"—love.

Why is love a more excellent way? Why is love deemed to be the best of all the alternative responses we can have toward others?

It's because God has made us this way. We know intuitively that it is much more precious and touching to be given something we need rather than going out and taking it for ourselves. The sandwich my wife makes for me tastes better than the one I scrounge together on my own. The meal my friend buys for me is a little sweeter than the lunch I picked up at the drive-thru on my way back to the office.

You may say, "No way, I'd rather get it myself!" Then you've exposed some hurts in your heart, because that's not how God has built you to work. Sure, a lot of people operate that way: "I can take care of myself. I don't need anybody!" But that's more a result of what life has done to them. It's not who they really are. God made us to spend our lives giving to others and being humble enough to receive their love in return. That's why Paul calls love the "more excellent way."

It's what we're made for.

Love is the litmus test of friendship—people who don't just hang around you when the band is playing but also when the music stops, not only when your popularity is soaring but when others turn against you. That's when you discover to your great relief that "a brother is born for a difficult time."

> A man with many friends may be harmed, but there is a friend who stays closer than a brother.
> PROVERBS 18:24

What incredible language! The people who are still there when life is tough and when friends are few are the ones who say, "Hey, are you having some hard times? Things aren't going so well? You've got some disappointments? Some things haven't come through for you? You've failed personally? You're struggling to go on? I was *born* for this!" True friends come alive at that time—standing with you, wanting to be there for you, saying to you, "I want to be your brother or sister in this difficult situation. I woke up this morning wanting to be a faithful friend to you."

I love that.

That's a friend. When others back away with their hands in their pockets, not really sure what to do, real friends move closer.

Even when human relationships fail, "there is a friend who stays closer than a brother." Solomon couldn't have known the full weight of what he was writing about at the time, but standing here thousands of years later, we know this "friend" to be Jesus Christ.

Many times I've let my friends down, and many times I've not been the example I needed to be—not every time, not all the time. Even when I am, there's a limit to how much we can draw down from our friends. But there is one Friend we can never ask too much of. Jesus knows us perfectly, loves us unconditionally, and is always available. He truly loves "at all times."

⊹

Wisdom Talking

When was the last time you experienced up-front, sacrificial love from a friend? Was it hard to receive? Or were you able to thank God for it? Who needs you to stand by them right now? How can you model Jesus' love in that relationship?

Day 24
Have Fun

Oil and incense bring joy to the heart, and the
sweetness of a friend is better than self-counsel.
Proverbs 27:9

I'm so glad the Word of God includes the
exhortation and encouragement to enjoy our friends.
We are not meant merely to sit beside each other's
hospital beds or to crowd into funeral homes. We
are not just to cry on their shoulders but to laugh at
their corny jokes, not just to share their pain but their
memories, too. Before Paul instructed us to "weep
with those who weep," he told us to "rejoice with
those who rejoice" (Rom. 12:15).

Friends are meant to have fun.

But not just idle, wasted, throw-away fun. Real
friends are the people who get past the PTA rumors
and the sale that's on at Target, past the missed
tackles in the Bears game and the latest stock market
results. Real friends are soul friends, people who can
talk to each other about heart matters. They're not
only around to shoot the breeze about surface stuff.
They also have fun giving each other hearty counsel,

sharing authentic matters of the soul. That's where the confidence comes from to open up your heart, to trust, to tell, to disclose without fear of a hasty conclusion or a harsh judgment. When you have a person to whom you can talk freely like that, you have a true friend.

A poem from the 1859 novel *A Life for a Life* by Dinah Maria Mulock Craik, says this: "Oh the comfort—the inexpressible comfort of feeling *safe* with a person—having neither to weigh thoughts or measure words, but pouring them all right out, just as they are, chaff and grain together, certain that a faithful hand will take and sift them, keep what is worth keeping, then with the breath of kindness, blow the rest away." If you have a friend like that, enjoy it as a genuine treasure. Delight in those friendships.

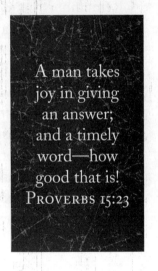

A man takes joy in giving an answer; and a timely word—how good that is!
PROVERBS 15:23

That's because sometimes, a friend is more valuable to us (in certain ways) than a family member. "Don't go to your brother's house in your time of calamity," Solomon advised. "Better a neighbor nearby then a brother far away" (Prov. 27:10). There's something about doing life together and growing in friendship that creates a bond between people greater even than blood. Many times, the people who care for you the most are not your sisters in Cleveland but the people you've come to know as godly friends.

I have three brothers, and I love them so deeply it's difficult for me to describe. I also have some brothers in the Lord who know me better now, who fellowship with me at a deeper level and provide greater support for me even than my own brothers.

Remember the story in Matthew 12 when Jesus' mother and siblings appeared at the door while he was teaching? People around him said, "Hey, Jesus, your family is outside." But Jesus responded, "Whoever does the will of My Father in heaven, that person is My brother and sister and mother" (Matt. 12:50). The bond of Christian fellowship and friendship often exceeds in depth and quality the nature of even good family relationships.

So enjoy your friends. Value their love and nearness and laughter. They are a gift from God to you.

Wisdom Talking

What are the things you and your friends most enjoy doing together? What makes their friendship so much fun? What about your friendship sets it apart from others?

Day 25
Guarded Treasure

A contrary man spreads conflict,
and a gossip separates friends.
Proverbs 16:28

Don't be a pervert.

"Uh, okay," you may say, a little smack of sarcasm in your voice. "I wasn't exactly planning on it."

In some translations of the verse above, the "contrary man" is said to be instead a "perverse man." Not the wild-eyed, drooling kind of sick-o, but one who for some twisted reason delights in stirring up trouble, in sowing conflict, in separating friends.

You can't spot this person right away. He's not the kind to drop a bomb in between people and be known as the perpetrator. Instead he "spreads conflict." He "sows strife," as some versions of the Bible say it. He plants little seeds that over time have the potential to grow into bigger issues with the muscle to push people apart, to arouse suspicions, to invite unkind words and actions. It's subtle. It's sneaky.

But they're out there, these perverts, bristling with the power to separate even the best of friends. They're not out in front where you can see them. They're off to the side, out in the parking lot, on the phone, at the store, over coffee, whispering things: "Did you hear about—? Can you believe it? Isn't it just awful? How could she do a thing like that?" Theirs is a condition born of insecurity, jealously, and anger, but it reveals itself in treachery and distrust.

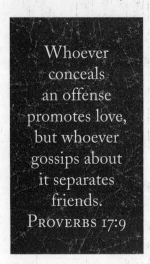

Whoever conceals an offense promotes love, but whoever gossips about it separates friends.

PROVERBS 17:9

Why would God put this verse in the Bible? Was he thinking that a perverse person would be reading the book of Proverbs, would slap himself in the forehead, and say, "Oh no, that's me! I've got to stop doing that!"

No, there's little likelihood that a foolish person is going to find much value in Proverbs, as if he was going to change anyway. This verse is for the person who wants to protect her friendships, who knows to be on the lookout for:

• *Bad reports.* "Hey, did you hear about such-and so? I know it's none of my business, but . . ."

• *Half truths.* "Did you hear that Bill lost his job? Did you hear why? I think the reason is . . ."

• *Exaggerations.* A kernel of truth expanded into a bad report.

• *Motive assessments.* "Do you know why she does that? You know why he acts that way?"

No, do you?

I've learned to stop this stuff in its tracks. If you're sincere about protecting your friendships, do these two things: 1) *stop the repetition* and 2) *cover the transgression.*

Bad reports may travel fast through the grapevine, but they need to stop with us. When people come up to me and say, "Pastor, did you know . . ." I usually answer back, "Why are you telling me this?" (That's a little nicer than saying what actually comes to mind: "What do my ears look like to you? A trash can?") This direct approach puts a strange, blank look on people's faces. "Why are you telling me this?" is the best reply I know of to a piece of gossip.

Only a few times in your life can you do something that you're absolutely sure God wants you to do. This is one of them. If you're serious about taking care of your friends, don't let the perverts have their way. "Hatred stirs up conflicts, but love covers all offenses" (Prov. 10:12).

✠

Wisdom Talking

Do bad reports stop with you, or do they continue on? Are you a clog or a conduit in the personal injury pipeline? What makes this a challenge in your life?

Day 26
Keeping It Real

The wounds of a friend are trustworthy,
but the kisses of an enemy are excessive.
Proverbs 27:6

Let's take one more day to look at friendship as seen in the book of Proverbs. Solomon gives us a challenge that far exceeds the greeting-card variety but, when placed in the right hands, can still have a Hallmark ending:

Be willing to tell your friends the truth.

Biblical friendship is not about pretending. It's not a case where we hypocritically pat each other on the back, kidding ourselves into believing that we have it all together. Let's skip the plastic compliments and the idea that we must avoid all discomfort if we're going to keep our friends. Real friends aren't afraid to develop each other—to give and receive the kind of frontline counsel that makes friendship the long-term blessing it can truly be.

Notice in the verse at the top of this page how the "enemy" is seen as the one giving the "kisses." We still use that same terminology today, only now we call it "kissing up." That's an enemy for you. "Oh, you're so great, you're the nicest person I've ever met, you're so funny, you're so smart, you're so good at so many things." Proverbs 27:14 says, "If one blesses his neighbor with a loud voice early in the morning, it will be counted as a curse to him." God's not saying that we shouldn't look for opportunities to be encouraging, that we shouldn't be quick to say nice things that build each other up. But the person who's always effusing these wonderful things non-stop is being cowardly in the matter of real friendship.

Don't rebuke a mocker, or he will hate you; rebuke a wise man, and he will love you.
PROVERBS 9:8

I'll admit to you, this doesn't really sound right at first. We think the Lord would be most pleased with us when we dish out the kindnesses, when we're gushing with positive things to say. But no, the compliments or "kisses" of a friend don't even get discussed here. The highest friend, the best friend—according to God's Word—is the friend who's willing to be wounded.

Yes, wounded. "The wounds of a friend."

If you've ever been on the receiving end of an honest word from someone who truly cared for you, then you know how "trustworthy" those wounds can be. Sure, they can sting for a while, but one day we find out just how valuable they are. On the other hand, the friend who does the wounding must be prepared to be injured as well. If we tell someone something difficult, even a good friend is liable to respond with, "I don't really want to hear this from you. What right do you have to point this out to me? Who do you think you are?" The answer is: "I'm a friend who loves you enough to tell you this hard thing even if you're going to hate me for saying it." That hurts. The friend who's willing to be wounded in order to get a piece of information through to you is a real friend.

Proverbs 27:17 says, "As iron sharpens iron, so a man sharpens the countenance of his friends." This is not two friends sipping milk shakes at McDonalds. This is intense. There's friction involved. Backs stiffen. Muscles flex. Sparks fly. But the result is growth and character, depth and purpose, richness and beauty.

It's all the things a friend really wants.

Wisdom Talking

How big of an investment have you been making lately in the lives of your friends? What could you begin doing to strengthen, sharpen, and challenge your friends?

Day 27
Sober Minded

It is not for kings, Lemuel, it is not for kings
to drink wine or for rulers to desire beer.
Proverbs 31:4

I'm going to take a couple of days to look at the matter of drinking—helping us wise up about alcohol—sharing with you what I believe the sum game of the Bible's wisdom to be on the subject:

Stay away from it. Totally.

It's not hard to recognize three types of people by their attitudes and behaviors toward alcohol: 1) those who completely abstain from it, 2) those who drink here and there primarily for relaxation or amusement, and 3) those who have a drinking problem. I don't know which would characterize you, but I'm convinced that total abstinence is the best and highest path for followers of Christ.

Don't worry—I'm not here to judge you. I hope that by the time you give this some consideration, instead of just backing into a lazy argument for why you think it's all right, you'll have a biblical basis for your defense. Fair warning? Okay, let's duke it out.

1) *Drunkenness is a sin, not a disease.* Yes, I know what the so-called experts say. The vast majority of Americans disagree with me on this. They would call me callously naïve and narrow-minded to make such a statement. But it's the only disease I know that can keep people out of heaven. The Bible says, "Do not be deceived: no sexually immoral people, idolaters,

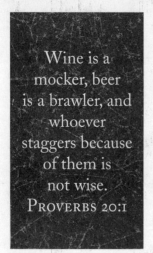

Wine is a mocker, beer is a brawler, and whoever staggers because of them is not wise.

PROVERBS 20:1

adulterers, male prostitutes, homosexuals, thieves, greedy people, *drunkards*, revilers, or swindlers will inherit God's kingdom" (1 Cor. 6:9–10). He doesn't mean we're doomed if we do it one time, but if we habitually commit these sins, it reveals that we're not following Jesus Christ and are therefore not headed for heaven.

Now, "some of you were like this" before Christ washed and saved you, as Paul said in the very next verse. Sure, we can have inclinations toward any or all of these sins, but inclination doesn't mean we can't resist. To see drunkenness listed alongside these other obvious deviations from Christian behavior should make us wonder why we're so tempted to give it the pass.

2) *Alcohol impairs wisdom.* Repeatedly in the Bible, those who held significant positions of responsibility were told to have nothing to do with alcohol. Too much was riding on their ability to make wise decisions.

Old Testament priests were forbidden alcohol (Lev. 10:9). Those who took the Nazirite vow to belong wholly to God were not to drink alcohol (Num. 6:3). In the New Testament, John the Baptist was forbidden alcohol (Luke 1:15). That's because alcohol impairs wisdom. If you've got a big job to do, you don't need 20 percent of your brain capacity flushed out of your system.

"But, hey, I'm no king or priest or anything," you may argue. You're not? If you're a Christian, you are. The Bible says that Jesus has "set us free from our sins by His blood, and made us a kingdom, priests to His God and Father" (Rev. 1:5–6).

You've got a monster task in front of you today, child of God, to represent your Lord and advance his kingdom on the earth. If that's not something you need a clear head for, I don't know what is.

Hey, alcohol impairs wisdom. Anybody got some wisdom they can do without today?

Wisdom Talking

What's your take on this controversial subject? Are you able to defend your position using God's Word to support your opinions? When have you chosen wisdom over freedom and regretted it?

Day 28
Woe and Whinery

Who has woe? . . . those who linger over wine,
those who go looking for mixed wine.
Proverbs 23:29–30

I believe the Bible teaches total abstinence from
alcohol, not because God is holding out on us but
because he has so much more for us. As we trust him
in matters of biblical truth and obey him as sold-out
servants of Jesus Christ, we find out more and more
how good and fully satisfying he really is.

Drinking can't do that for us. It can't give us what
we really want or need. It can, however, always be
counted on for the following:

1) *Alcohol is destructive.* We know it kills brain cells,
leads to sluggish thinking, and contributes heavily to
obesity, liver disease, and heart conditions. Drinking is
famously known as a leading cause of traffic accidents
(and of course, deaths), family breakdown, and child
abuse. Alcohol and violence often go hand in hand.
It's in the papers every single day.

Solomon knew about these destructive tendencies.
He knew that alcohol "bites like a snake and stings

like a viper" (Prov. 23:32). It's not like a bear that you can see coming toward you. Instead, it's fast and deadly. It quickly becomes large and irreversible. If there's anything I've observed from working with alcoholics my entire adult life, it's that they are the last ones to figure out they have a problem. Something in alcohol consumes one's capacity to discern that he's lost control. Wise people don't say, "I wonder how close I can get to the edge and not lose it?" Soon enough, alcohol spills over into loss and destruction.

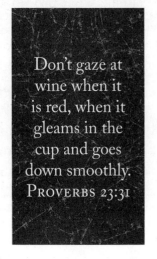

Don't gaze at wine when it is red, when it gleams in the cup and goes down smoothly.
PROVERBS 23:31

2) *Alcohol is addictive.* That's the point of Proverbs 23:35— "They struck me, but I feel no pain! They beat me, but I didn't know it! When will I wake up? I'll look for another drink." No matter how many warnings go off in your head, the further you get into alcohol, the harder it is to extricate yourself.

I don't know how many times I've seen the cycle take place. It starts with a choice to change. Soon after, the physical desire to drink overwhelms them, and back they go to the bottle. The shame, the self-hatred, and—again—the desire to change. Around and around it goes, the downward spiral. Why would a follower of Christ, a blood-bought servant of the living God, involve himself with something that has attached to it this kind of deception and heaviness?

3) *Wisdom calls us to set it aside.* The book of Proverbs teaches that abstinence from alcohol is a wise choice. But Romans 14 affirms it even more:

It is a *loving choice*, "for if your brother is hurt by what you eat [or drink], you are no longer walking according to love" (v. 15).

It is an *edifying choice*—verse 19 says, "We must pursue what promotes peace and what builds up one another."

It is also a *supportive choice*, since "it is a noble thing not to eat meat, or drink wine, or do anything that makes your brother stumble" (v. 21). We don't live the Christian life for ourselves but for God and for others. Wisdom and love instruct us to live in a way that exceeds bare-bones obedience.

Some would say my stance is mere legalism and self-imposed denial. I say it's a matter of freedom.

Wisdom Talking

What would be clearer in your relationship with Christ if you didn't have the added burden of alcohol between you?

Day 29
So Satisfying

Wisdom resides in the heart of the discerning;
she is known even among fools.
Proverbs 14:33

You may be thinking that all this talk about wisdom is too little, too late. It may sound so far above and beyond you right now, there's no way in the world you can see yourself attaining it.

Why even try?

Perhaps you've got all you can do just to hold your own life together. Perhaps you've failed so badly and so profoundly, you don't see any way out. Perhaps you're long past giving up hope of being rescued from the problems you've caused or the circumstances you've found yourself in.

God's Word is here to tell you that his wisdom is available both to stabilize and to satisfy you. It's not too late, it's not too far away, it's not impossible to contemplate your life taking a turn for the better. But if it does, it will do so only on the strong back of God's wisdom, as he leads you to make sound choices and eternally-minded decisions.

One of the things wisdom offers you is the ability *to rest in God's timing and provision.* I love that word picture from the verse on the previous page—wisdom "resides" or "rests" in the heart of the wise person. He's not always running around, desperate and out of breath. He doesn't feel constantly lost and misplaced. He isn't jabbering his head off, full of foolishness

Wisdom . . .
If you find it
you will have
a future, and
your hope will
never fade.
PROVERBS 24:14

yet never at a loss for words. Instead, he's at home within himself and in his relationship with God. He's at rest, quieting himself.

Fools, on the other hand, are always shooting off their mouths, causing great injury to themselves and others. Even believers can be guilty of this, wanting to be bold in sharing their faith but never waiting on a nudge from the Holy Spirit, usually barging in without thinking and busting up the place. In wisdom, there is stability—the settled knowledge that God is at work, and therefore we can wait. We can rest in that.

Wisdom also promises *to satisfy and bring hope in its wake.* Proverbs 24:13–14 basically says, "What honey is to the mouth, wisdom is to the soul." It's sweet and satisfying. It helps us believe and appropriate the promises of God that assure us we have a hope and a future with him.

Often in life, we think we've irreparably blown it. We've made a mistake that's left us no retreat, no chance of getting to a good place anymore. But as long as there is wisdom—a desire to learn and grow from our mistakes—there is hope.

Hopelessness comes, not just from having failed, but from having failed with no clue about how to get to a better place. The hopeless people in our world are those who don't have any idea how to get anywhere else than where they are.

But in the wonderful provision of God's Word, no matter how many times we fall or fail, we read there's always the chance to learn and grow and implement his wisdom into our life. It's like honey in our mouth, the promise of good things to come, of restoration and blessing. That's the prospect, the heritage, the God-given legacy of the wise.

That can be you, sooner than you think.

Wisdom Talking

Think of someone right now who could shoot straight with you about your current situation and could share God's hope with you. Make plans to talk.

Day 30
Listen Up

A wise man will listen and increase his learning,
and a discerning man will obtain guidance.
Proverbs 1:5

Okay. So you want to have a heart of wisdom? You want to grow in your ability to walk with a steady pace through life? Then I'll close our time together by just sharing two final things from the Proverbs—two things that, if we'll do them faithfully and consistently, will open the door for God to build some amazing muscles in our lives.

1. *Listen to wise people.* That sounds pretty obvious, right? But how do you know a wise person when you see one? How can you be fairly sure that it's wisdom you're getting when you talk to him? Not everyone who claims to have wisdom is really wise. I observe people all the time going to non-Christians for advice, who can do no more than counsel to their flesh. "I would do this, I would do that. You're not going to take that anymore, are you?" They spout worldly, self-centered nonsense instead of sharing God's heart of wisdom. Don't listen to that.

How do you know the difference? Jesus (as always) sets the model for us. Whenever people went to him and asked, "What should we do? Is this right? How can we know the truth?" he would answer, "It is written." As many as twenty-five times in the Gospels, we hear Jesus say this or some version of it.

You'll know you're talking to a wise person when he can't get halfway through the first paragraph without letting you know that he doesn't have any wisdom at all, but that all of his wisdom comes from God and his Word. I've gone to people for counsel whose lips just dripped the Word of God, whose wisdom was so obviously God's and not the world's.

> The fear of the Lord is the beginning of wisdom, and the knowledge of the Holy One is understanding.
> PROVERBS 9:10

A person may appear wise, but if he's not constantly taking us back to Scripture while he's talking, he is filled up with foolishness.

When you find a wise person, be sure to listen. The number one indication of a bright spiritual future is a teachable spirit. Because my ministry is teaching God's Word, I get a great many opportunities to see the difference. Unteachable people will walk up to me, give me a note, itching to debate and wrestle with me, changing the subject. But when you get around people who are wise, open up your ears. Listen. Then put what they say to work in your life.

2. *Seek the Holy One.* "The knowledge of the Holy One is understanding." I used to think this was only referring to God, but I discovered that "Holy One" is mentioned fifty-seven times in the Bible. It refers to someone preparing for a day of judgment but who loves people. Sound like Jesus to you? When the angel said to Mary, "The holy One to be born will be called the Son of God" (Luke 1:35), he left no doubt who he was talking about.

You want wisdom? Be like the wise men who came from the East. We don't really know much about them. Most of the ways we see them portrayed in the Christmas pageants are pure conjecture. We know for sure that they were seeking wisdom by seeking a king, by seeking the Holy One.

None of us know it all, but we all have a place to go to find it. It's available from God free of charge, though not free of effort and desire. Get wisdom!

Wisdom Talking

What are the main things God has shown you in this brief look at wisdom? Develop an action plan to bring specific application to your life in these areas. Decide what needs to change, what can be nurtured, what to do today.

Proverbs

The Purpose of Proverbs

1 The proverbs of Solomon son of David,
king of Israel:

2 For gaining wisdom and being instructed;
for understanding insightful sayings;

3 for receiving wise instruction
in righteousness, justice, and integrity;

4 for teaching shrewdness to the inexperienced,
knowledge and discretion to a young man—

5 a wise man will listen and increase his learning,
and a discerning man will obtain guidance—

6 for understanding a proverb or a parable,
the words of the wise, and their riddles.

7 The fear of the LORD
is the beginning of knowledge;
fools despise wisdom and instruction.

Avoid the Path of the Violent

8 Listen, my son, to your father's instruction,
and don't reject your mother's teaching,

9 for they will be a garland of grace on your head
and a gold chain around your neck.

10 My son, if sinners entice you,
don't be persuaded.

11 If they say—"Come with us!
Let's set an ambush and kill someone.
Let's attack some innocent person just for fun!

12 Let's swallow them alive, like Sheol,
still healthy as they go down to the Pit.

13 We'll find all kinds of valuable property
and fill our houses with plunder.

14 Throw in your lot with us,
and we'll all share our money"—

15   my son, don't travel that road with them
     or set foot on their path,
16   because their feet run toward trouble
     and they hurry to commit murder.
17   It is foolish to spread a net
     where any bird can see it,
18   but they set an ambush to kill themselves;
     they attack their own lives.
19   Such are the paths of all who pursue
     gain dishonestly;
     it takes the lives of those who profit from it.

Wisdom's Plea

20   Wisdom calls out in the street;
     she raises her voice in the public squares.
21   She cries out above the commotion;
     she speaks at the entrance of the city gates:
22   "How long, foolish ones, will you love ignorance?
     How long will you mockers enjoy mocking
     and you fools hate knowledge?
23   If you turn to my discipline,
     then I will pour out my spirit on you
     and teach you my words.
24   Since I called out and you refused,
     extended my hand and no one paid attention,
25   since you neglected all my counsel
     and did not accept my correction,
26   I, in turn, will laugh at your calamity.
     I will mock when terror strikes you,
27   when terror strikes you like a storm
     and your calamity comes like a whirlwind,
     when trouble and stress overcome you.
28   Then they will call me, but I won't answer;
     they will search for me, but won't find me.
29   Because they hated knowledge,
     didn't choose to fear the LORD,
30   were not interested in my counsel,
     and rejected all my correction,

31   they will eat the fruit of their way
and be glutted with their own schemes.
32   For the waywardness of the inexperienced
will kill them,
and the complacency of fools will destroy them.
33   But whoever listens to me will live securely
and be free from the fear of danger."

Wisdom's Worth

2   My son, if you accept my words
and store up my commands within you,
2   listening closely to wisdom
and directing your heart to understanding;
3   furthermore, if you call out to insight
and lift your voice to understanding,
4   if you seek it like silver
and search for it like hidden treasure,
5   then you will understand the fear of the LORD
and discover the knowledge of God.
6   For the LORD gives wisdom;
from His mouth come knowledge
and understanding.
7   He stores up success for the upright;
He is a shield for those who live with integrity
8   so that He may guard the paths of justice
and protect the way of His loyal followers.
9   Then you will understand righteousness, justice,
and integrity—every good path.
10   For wisdom will enter your mind,
and knowledge will delight your heart.
11   Discretion will watch over you,
and understanding will guard you,
12   rescuing you from the way of evil—
from the one who says perverse things,
13   from those who abandon the right paths
to walk in ways of darkness,
14   from those who enjoy doing evil
and celebrate perversity,

15 whose paths are crooked,
   and whose ways are devious.
16 It will rescue you from a forbidden woman,
   from a stranger with her flattering talk,
17 who abandons the companion of her youth
   and forgets the covenant of her God;
18 for her house sinks down to death
   and her ways to the land of the departed spirits.
19 None return who go to her;
   none reach the paths of life.
20 So follow the way of good people,
   and keep to the paths of the righteous.
21 For the upright will inhabit the land,
   and those of integrity will remain in it;
22 but the wicked will be cut off from the land,
   and the treacherous uprooted from it.

Trust the LORD

3 My son, don't forget my teaching,
   but let your heart keep my commands;
2 for they will bring you
   many days, a full life, and well-being.
3 Never let loyalty and faithfulness leave you.
   Tie them around your neck;
   write them on the tablet of your heart.
4 Then you will find favor and high regard
   in the sight of God and man.
5 Trust in the LORD with all your heart,
   and do not rely on your own understanding;
6 think about Him in all your ways,
   and He will guide you on the right paths.
7 Don't consider yourself to be wise;
   fear the LORD and turn away from evil.
8 This will be healing for your body
   and strengthening for your bones.
9 Honor the LORD with your possessions
   and with the first produce of your entire harvest;
10 then your barns will be completely filled,

and your vats will overflow with new wine.

11 Do not despise the LORD's instruction, my son,
and do not loathe His discipline;
12 for the LORD disciplines the one He loves,
just as a father, the son he delights in.

Wisdom Brings Happiness

13 Happy is a man who finds wisdom
and who acquires understanding,
14 for she is more profitable than silver,
and her revenue is better than gold.
15 She is more precious than jewels;
nothing you desire compares with her.
16 Long life is in her right hand;
in her left, riches and honor.
17 Her ways are pleasant,
and all her paths, peaceful.
18 She is a tree of life to those who embrace her,
and those who hold on to her are happy.
19 The LORD founded the earth by wisdom
and established the heavens by understanding.
20 By His knowledge the watery depths broke open,
and the clouds dripped with dew.
21 Maintain your competence and discretion.
My son, don't lose sight of them.
22 They will be life for you
and adornment for your neck.
23 Then you will go safely on your way;
your foot will not stumble.
24 When you lie down, you will not be afraid;
you will lie down, and your sleep will be pleasant.
25 Don't fear sudden danger
or the ruin of the wicked when it comes,
26 for the LORD will be your confidence
and will keep your foot from a snare.

Treat Others Fairly

27 When it is in your power,
don't withhold good from the one to whom

it is due.
28 Don't say to your neighbor, "Go away!
Come back later.
I'll give it tomorrow"—when it is there with you.
29 Don't plan any harm against your neighbor,
for he trusts you and lives near you.
30 Don't accuse anyone without cause,
when he has done you no harm.
31 Don't envy a violent man
or choose any of his ways;
32 for the devious are detestable to the Lord,
but He is a friend to the upright.
33 The Lord's curse is on the household
of the wicked,
but He blesses the home of the righteous;
34 He mocks those who mock,
but gives grace to the humble.
35 The wise will inherit honor,
but He holds up fools to dishonor.

A Father's Example

4 Listen, my sons, to a father's discipline,
and pay attention so that
you may gain understanding,
2 for I am giving you good instruction.
Don't abandon my teaching.
3 When I was a son with my father,
tender and precious to my mother,
4 he taught me and said:
"Your heart must hold on to my words.
Keep my commands and live.
5 Get wisdom, get understanding;
don't forget or turn away from the words
of my mouth.
6 Don't abandon wisdom, and she will
watch over you;
love her, and she will guard you.
7 Wisdom is supreme—so get wisdom.

And whatever else you get, get understanding.

8 Cherish her, and she will exalt you;
if you embrace her, she will honor you.

9 She will place a garland of grace on your head;
she will give you a crown of beauty."

Two Ways of Life

10 Listen, my son. Accept my words,
and you will live many years.

11 I am teaching you the way of wisdom;
I am guiding you on straight paths.

12 When you walk, your steps will not be hindered;
when you run, you will not stumble.

13 Hold on to instruction; don't let go.
Guard it, for it is your life.

14 Don't set foot on the path of the wicked;
don't proceed in the way of evil ones.

15 Avoid it; don't travel on it.
Turn away from it, and pass it by.

16 For they can't sleep
unless they have done what is evil;
they are robbed of sleep unless they make
someone stumble.

17 They eat the bread of wickedness
and drink the wine of violence.

18 The path of the righteous is like the light of dawn,
shining brighter and brighter until midday.

19 But the way of the wicked is
like the darkest gloom;
they don't know what makes them stumble.

The Straight Path

20 My son, pay attention to my words;
listen closely to my sayings.

21 Don't lose sight of them;
keep them within your heart.

22 For they are life to those who find them,
and health to one's whole body.

23 Guard your heart above all else,

for it is the source of life.

24 Don't let your mouth speak dishonestly,
and don't let your lips talk deviously.

25 Let your eyes look forward;
fix your gaze straight ahead.

26 Carefully consider the path for your feet,
and all your ways will be established.

27 Don't turn to the right or to the left;
keep your feet away from evil.

Avoid Seduction

5 My son, pay attention to my wisdom;
listen closely to my understanding

2 so that you may maintain discretion
and your lips safeguard knowledge.

3 Though the lips of the forbidden woman
drip honey
and her words are smoother than oil,

4 in the end she's as bitter as wormwood
and as sharp as a double-edged sword.

5 Her feet go down to death;
her steps head straight for Sheol.

6 She doesn't consider the path of life;
she doesn't know that her ways are unstable.

7 So now, my sons, listen to me,
and don't turn away from the words of my mouth.

8 Keep your way far from her.
Don't go near the door of her house.

9 Otherwise, you will give up your vitality to others
and your years to someone cruel;

10 strangers will drain your resources,
and your earnings will end up
in a foreigner's house.

11 At the end of your life, you will lament
when your physical body has been consumed,

12 and you will say, "How I hated discipline,
and how my heart despised correction.

13 I didn't obey my teachers

or listen closely to my mentors.

14 I was on the verge of complete ruin
before the entire community."

Enjoy Marriage

15 Drink water from your own cistern,
water flowing from your own well.

16 Should your springs flow in the streets,
streams of water in the public squares?

17 They should be for you alone
and not for you to share with strangers.

18 Let your fountain be blessed,
and take pleasure in the wife of your youth.

19 A loving doe, a graceful fawn—
let her breasts always satisfy you;
be lost in her love forever.

20 Why, my son, would you be infatuated
with a forbidden woman
or embrace the breast of a stranger?

21 For a man's ways are before the LORD's eyes,
and He considers all his paths.

22 A wicked man's iniquities entrap him;
he is entangled in the ropes of his own sin.

23 He will die because there is no instruction,
and be lost because of his great stupidity.

Financial Entanglements

6 My son, if you have put up security
for your neighbor
or entered into an agreement with a stranger,

2 you have been trapped by the words of your lips—
ensnared by the words of your mouth.

3 Do this, then, my son, and free yourself,
for you have put yourself in your neighbor's power:
Go, humble yourself, and plead
with your neighbor.

4 Don't give sleep to your eyes
or slumber to your eyelids.

⁵ Escape like a gazelle from a hunter,
like a bird from a fowler's trap.

Laziness

⁶ Go to the ant, you slacker!
Observe its ways and become wise.
⁷ Without leader, administrator, or ruler,
⁸ it prepares its provisions in summer;
it gathers its food during harvest.
⁹ How long will you stay in bed, you slacker?
When will you get up from your sleep?
¹⁰ A little sleep, a little slumber,
a little folding of the arms to rest,
¹¹ and your poverty will come like a robber,
your need, like a bandit.

The Malicious Man

¹² A worthless person, a wicked man,
who goes around speaking dishonestly,
¹³ who winks his eyes, signals with his feet,
and gestures with his fingers,
¹⁴ who plots evil with perversity in his heart—
he stirs up trouble constantly.
¹⁵ Therefore calamity will strike him suddenly;
he will be shattered instantly—beyond recovery.

What the LORD Hates

¹⁶ Six things the LORD hates;
in fact, seven are detestable to Him:
¹⁷ arrogant eyes, a lying tongue,
hands that shed innocent blood,
¹⁸ a heart that plots wicked schemes,
feet eager to run to evil,
¹⁹ a lying witness who gives false testimony,
and one who stirs up trouble among brothers.

Warning against Adultery

²⁰ My son, keep your father's command,
and don't reject your mother's teaching.

21 Always bind them to your heart;
tie them around your neck.
22 When you walk here and there, they will
guide you;
when you lie down, they will watch over you;
when you wake up, they will talk to you.
23 For a commandment is a lamp, teaching is a light,
and corrective instructions are the way to life.
24 They will protect you from an evil woman,
from the flattering tongue of a stranger.
25 Don't lust in your heart for her beauty
or let her captivate you with her eyelashes.
26 For a prostitute's fee is only a loaf of bread,
but an adulteress goes after your very life.
27 Can a man embrace fire
and his clothes not be burned?
28 Can a man walk on coals
without scorching his feet?
29 So it is with the one who sleeps with
another man's wife;
no one who touches her will go unpunished.
30 People don't despise the thief if he steals
to satisfy himself when he is hungry.
31 Still, if caught, he must pay seven times as much;
he must give up all the wealth in his house.
32 The one who commits adultery lacks sense;
whoever does so destroys himself.
33 He will get a beating and dishonor,
and his disgrace will never be removed.
34 For jealousy enrages a husband,
and he will show no mercy
when he takes revenge.
35 He will not be appeased by anything
or be persuaded by lavish gifts.

7 My son, obey my words,
and treasure my commands.
2 Keep my commands and live;
protect my teachings

as you would the pupil of your eye.
3   Tie them to your fingers;
    write them on the tablet of your heart.
4   Say to wisdom, "You are my sister,"
    and call understanding your relative.
5   She will keep you from a forbidden woman,
    a stranger with her flattering talk.

A Story of Seduction

6   At the window of my house
    I looked through my lattice.
7   I saw among the inexperienced,
    I noticed among the youths,
    a young man lacking sense.
8   Crossing the street near her corner,
    he strolled down the road to her house
9   at twilight, in the evening,
    in the dark of the night.
10 A woman came to meet him,
    dressed like a prostitute,
    having a hidden agenda.
11 She is loud and defiant;
    her feet do not stay at home.
12 Now in the street, now in the squares,
    she lurks at every corner.
13 She grabs him and kisses him;
    she brazenly says to him,
14 "I've made fellowship offerings;
    today I've fulfilled my vows.
15 So I came out to meet you,
    to search for you, and I've found you.
16 I've spread coverings on my bed—
    richly colored linen from Egypt.
17 I've perfumed my bed
    with myrrh, aloes, and cinnamon.
18 Come, let's drink deeply of lovemaking
    until morning.
    Let's feast on each other's love!

¹⁹ My husband isn't home;
he went on a long journey.
²⁰ He took a bag of money with him
and will come home at the time of the full moon."
²¹ She seduces him with her persistent pleading;
she lures with her flattering talk.
²² He follows her impulsively
like an ox going to the slaughter,
like a deer bounding toward a trap
²³ until an arrow pierces its liver,
like a bird darting into a snare—
he doesn't know it will cost him his life.
²⁴ Now, my sons, listen to me,
and pay attention to the words of my mouth.
²⁵ Don't let your heart turn aside to her ways;
don't stray onto her paths.
²⁶ For she has brought many down to death;
her victims are countless.
²⁷ Her house is the road to Sheol,
descending to the chambers of death.

Wisdom's Appeal

8 Doesn't Wisdom call out?
Doesn't Understanding make her voice heard?
² At the heights overlooking the road,
at the crossroads, she takes her stand.
³ Beside the gates at the entry to the city,
at the main entrance, she cries out:
⁴ "People, I call out to you;
my cry is to mankind.
⁵ Learn to be shrewd, you who are inexperienced;
develop common sense, you who are foolish.
⁶ Listen, for I speak of noble things,
and what my lips say is right.
⁷ For my mouth tells the truth,
and wickedness is detestable to my lips.
⁸ All the words of my mouth are righteous;
none of them are deceptive or perverse.

⁹ All of them are clear to the perceptive,
and right to those who discover knowledge.
¹⁰ Accept my instruction instead of silver,
and knowledge rather than pure gold.
¹¹ For wisdom is better than precious stones,
and nothing desirable can compare with it.
¹² I, Wisdom, share a home with shrewdness
and have knowledge and discretion.
¹³ To fear the LORD is to hate evil.
I hate arrogant pride, evil conduct,
and perverse speech.
¹⁴ I possess good advice and competence;
I have understanding and strength.
¹⁵ It is by me that kings reign
and rulers enact just law;
¹⁶ by me, princes lead,
as do nobles and all righteous judges.
¹⁷ I love those who love me,
and those who search for me find me.
¹⁸ With me are riches and honor,
lasting wealth and righteousness.
¹⁹ My fruit is better than solid gold,
and my harvest than pure silver.
²⁰ I walk in the way of righteousness,
along the paths of justice,
²¹ giving wealth as an inheritance to those
who love me,
and filling their treasuries.
²² The LORD made me
at the beginning of His creation,
before His works of long ago.
²³ I was formed before ancient times,
from the beginning, before the earth began.
²⁴ I was brought forth
when there were no watery depths
and no springs filled with water.
²⁵ I was brought forth
before the mountains and hills were established,

26 before He made the land, the fields,
or the first soil on earth.
27 I was there when He established the heavens,
when He laid out the horizon on the surface
of the ocean,
28 when He placed the skies above,
when the fountains of the ocean gushed forth,
29 when He set a limit for the sea
so that the waters would not violate His command,
when He laid out the foundations of the earth.
30 I was a skilled craftsman beside Him.
I was His delight every day,
always rejoicing before Him.
31 I was rejoicing in His inhabited world,
delighting in the human race.
32 And now, my sons, listen to me;
those who keep my ways are happy.
33 Listen to instruction and be wise;
don't ignore it.
34 Anyone who listens to me is happy,
watching at my doors every day,
waiting by the posts of my doorway.
35 For the one who finds me finds life
and obtains favor from the LORD,
36 but the one who sins against me harms himself;
all who hate me love death."

Wisdom versus Foolishness

9 Wisdom has built her house;
she has carved out her seven pillars.
2 She has prepared her meat; she has mixed
her wine;
she has also set her table.
3 She has sent out her servants;
she calls out from the highest points of the city:
4 "Whoever is inexperienced, enter here!"
To the one who lacks sense, she says,
5 "Come, eat my bread,

and drink the wine I have mixed.

⁶ Leave inexperience behind, and you will live;
pursue the way of understanding.

⁷ The one who corrects a mocker
will bring dishonor on himself;
the one who rebukes a wicked man will get hurt.

⁸ Don't rebuke a mocker, or he will hate you;
rebuke a wise man, and he will love you.

⁹ Instruct a wise man, and he will be wiser still;
teach a righteous man, and he will learn more.

¹⁰ The fear of the LORD is the beginning of wisdom,
and the knowledge of the Holy One
is understanding.

¹¹ For by Wisdom your days will be many,
and years will be added to your life.

¹² If you are wise, you are wise for your own benefit;
if you mock, you alone will bear
the consequences."

¹³ The woman Folly is rowdy;
she is gullible and knows nothing.

¹⁴ She sits by the doorway of her house,
on a seat at the highest point of the city,

¹⁵ calling to those who pass by,
who go straight ahead on their paths:

¹⁶ "Whoever is inexperienced, enter here!"
To the one who lacks sense, she says,

¹⁷ "Stolen water is sweet,
and bread eaten secretly is tasty!"

¹⁸ But he doesn't know that the departed spirits
are there,
that her guests are in the depths of Sheol.

A Collection of Solomon's Proverbs

10 Solomon's proverbs:

A wise son brings joy to his father,
but a foolish son, heartache to his mother.

² Ill-gotten gains do not profit anyone,

but righteousness rescues from death.

3   The Lord will not let the righteous go hungry,
but He denies the wicked what they crave.

4   Idle hands make one poor,
but diligent hands bring riches.

5   The son who gathers during summer is prudent;
the son who sleeps during harvest is disgraceful.

6   Blessings are on the head of the righteous,
but the mouth of the wicked conceals violence.

7   The remembrance of the righteous is a blessing,
but the name of the wicked will rot.

8   A wise heart accepts commands,
but foolish lips will be destroyed.

9   The one who lives with integrity lives securely,
but whoever perverts his ways will be found out.

10   A sly wink of the eye causes grief,
and foolish lips will be destroyed.

11   The mouth of the righteous is a fountain of life,
but the mouth of the wicked conceals violence.

12   Hatred stirs up conflicts,
but love covers all offenses.

13   Wisdom is found on the lips of the discerning,
but a rod is for the back of the one
who lacks sense.

14   The wise store up knowledge,
but the mouth of the fool hastens destruction.

15   A rich man's wealth is his fortified city;
the poverty of the poor is their destruction.

16   The labor of the righteous leads to life;
the activity of the wicked leads to sin.

17   The one who follows instruction is on the path
to life,

but the one who rejects correction goes astray.

18 The one who conceals hatred has lying lips,
and whoever spreads slander is a fool.

19 When there are many words, sin is unavoidable,
but the one who controls his lips is wise.

20 The tongue of the righteous is pure silver;
the heart of the wicked is of little value.

21 The lips of the righteous feed many,
but fools die for lack of sense.

22 The LORD's blessing enriches,
and struggle adds nothing to it.

23 As shameful conduct is pleasure for a fool,
so wisdom is for a man of understanding.

24 What the wicked dreads will come to him,
but what the righteous desires will be given
to him.

25 When the whirlwind passes,
the wicked are no more,
but the righteous are secure forever.

26 Like vinegar to the teeth and smoke to the eyes,
so the slacker is to the one who sends him
on an errand.

27 The fear of the LORD prolongs life,
but the years of the wicked are cut short.

28 The hope of the righteous is joy,
but the expectation of the wicked
comes to nothing.

29 The way of the LORD is a stronghold
for the honorable,
but destruction awaits the malicious.

30 The righteous will never be shaken,
but the wicked will not remain on the earth.

31 The mouth of the righteous produces wisdom,

but a perverse tongue will be cut out.

32 The lips of the righteous know what is appropriate,
but the mouth of the wicked, only
what is perverse.

11 Dishonest scales are detestable to the LORD,
but an accurate weight is His delight.

2 When pride comes, disgrace follows,
but with humility comes wisdom.

3 The integrity of the upright guides them,
but the perversity of the treacherous
destroys them.

4 Wealth is not profitable on a day of wrath,
but righteousness rescues from death.

5 The righteousness of the blameless clears his path,
but the wicked person will fall because of
his wickedness.

6 The righteousness of the upright rescues them,
but the treacherous are trapped by
their own desires.

7 When the wicked dies,
his expectation comes to nothing,
and hope placed in wealth vanishes.

8 The righteous is rescued from trouble;
in his place, the wicked goes in.

9 With his mouth the ungodly destroys his neighbor,
but through knowledge the righteous are rescued.

10 When the righteous thrive, a city rejoices,
and when the wicked die, there is joyful shouting.

11 A city is built up by the blessing of the upright,
but it is torn down by the mouth of the wicked.

12 Whoever shows contempt for his neighbor
lacks sense,
but a man with understanding keeps silent.

13 A gossip goes around revealing a secret,
but the trustworthy keeps a confidence.

14 Without guidance, people fall,
but with many counselors there is deliverance.

15 If someone puts up security for a stranger,
he will suffer for it,
but the one who hates such agreements
is protected.

16 A gracious woman gains honor,
but violent men gain only riches.

17 A kind man benefits himself,
but a cruel man brings disaster on himself.

18 The wicked man earns an empty wage,
but the one who sows righteousness,
a true reward.

19 Genuine righteousness leads to life,
but pursuing evil leads to death.

20 Those with twisted minds are detestable
to the LORD,
but those with blameless conduct are His delight.

21 Be assured that the wicked
will not go unpunished,
but the offspring of the righteous will escape.

22 A beautiful woman who rejects good sense
is like a gold ring in a pig's snout.

23 The desire of the righteous turns out well,
but the hope of the wicked leads to wrath.

24 One person gives freely,
yet gains more;
another withholds what is right,
only to become poor.

25 A generous person will be enriched,
and the one who gives a drink of water

will receive water.

26 People will curse anyone who hoards grain,
but a blessing will come to the one who sells it.

27 The one who searches for what is good finds favor,
but if someone looks for trouble, it will come
to him.

28 Anyone trusting in his riches will fall,
but the righteous will flourish like foliage.

29 The one who brings ruin on his household
will inherit the wind,
and a fool will be a slave
to someone whose heart is wise.

30 The fruit of the righteous is a tree of life,
but violence takes lives.

31 If the righteous will be repaid on earth,
how much more the wicked and sinful.

12 Whoever loves instruction loves knowledge,
but one who hates correction is stupid.

2 The good obtain favor from the Lord,
but He condemns a man who schemes.

3 Man cannot be made secure by wickedness,
but the root of the righteous is immovable.

4 A capable wife is her husband's crown,
but a wife who causes shame
is like rottenness in his bones.

5 The thoughts of the righteous are just,
but guidance from the wicked leads to deceit.

6 The words of the wicked are a deadly ambush,
but the speech of the upright rescues them.

7 The wicked are overthrown and perish,
but the house of the righteous will stand.

8 A man is praised for his insight,

but a twisted mind is despised.

9 Better to be dishonored, yet have a servant,
than to act important but have no food.

10 A righteous man cares about his animal's health,
but even the merciful acts of the wicked are cruel.

11 The one who works his land will have plenty
of food,
but whoever chases fantasies lacks sense.

12 The wicked desire what evil men have,
but the root of the righteous produces fruit.

13 An evil man is trapped by his rebellious speech,
but the righteous escapes from trouble.

14 A man will be satisfied with good
by the words of his mouth,
and the work of a man's hands will reward him.

15 A fool's way is right in his own eyes,
but whoever listens to counsel is wise.

16 A fool's displeasure is known at once,
but whoever ignores an insult is sensible.

17 Whoever speaks the truth declares what is right,
but a false witness, deceit.

18 There is one who speaks rashly,
like a piercing sword;
but the tongue of the wise brings healing.

19 Truthful lips endure forever,
but a lying tongue, only a moment.

20 Deceit is in the hearts of those who plot evil,
but those who promote peace have joy.

21 No disaster overcomes the righteous,
but the wicked are full of misery.

22 Lying lips are detestable to the LORD,
but faithful people are His delight.

23   A shrewd person conceals knowledge,
but a foolish heart publicizes stupidity.

24   The diligent hand will rule,
but laziness will lead to forced labor.

25   Anxiety in a man's heart weighs it down,
but a good word cheers it up.

26   A righteous man is careful in dealing
with his neighbor,
but the ways of wicked men lead them astray.

27   A lazy man doesn't roast his game,
but to a diligent man, his wealth is precious.

28   There is life in the path of righteousness,
but another path leads to death.

13   A wise son hears his father's instruction,
but a mocker doesn't listen to rebuke.

2   From the words of his mouth,
a man will enjoy good things,
but treacherous people have an appetite
for violence.

3   The one who guards his mouth protects his life;
the one who opens his lips invites his own ruin.

4   The slacker craves, yet has nothing,
but the diligent is fully satisfied.

5   The righteous hate lying,
but the wicked act disgustingly and disgracefully.

6   Righteousness guards people of integrity,
but wickedness undermines the sinner.

7   One man pretends to be rich but has nothing;
another pretends to be poor but has great wealth.

8   Riches are a ransom for a man's life,
but a poor man hears no threat.

9   The light of the righteous shines brightly,

but the lamp of the wicked is extinguished.

10 Arrogance leads to nothing but strife,
but wisdom is gained by those who take advice.

11 Wealth obtained by fraud will dwindle,
but whoever earns it through labor will multiply it.

12 Delayed hope makes the heart sick,
but fulfilled desire is a tree of life.

13 The one who has contempt for instruction will pay
the penalty,
but the one who respects a command
will be rewarded.

14 A wise man's instruction is a fountain of life,
turning people away from the snares of death.

15 Good sense wins favor,
but the way of the treacherous never changes.

16 Every sensible person acts knowledgeably,
but a fool displays his stupidity.

17 A wicked messenger falls into trouble,
but a trustworthy courier brings healing.

18 Poverty and disgrace come to those
who ignore instruction,
but the one who accepts rebuke will be honored.

19 Desire fulfilled is sweet to the taste,
but fools hate to turn from evil.

20 The one who walks with the wise
will become wise,
but a companion of fools will suffer harm.

21 Disaster pursues sinners,
but good rewards the righteous.

22 A good man leaves an inheritance to his
grandchildren,
but the sinner's wealth is stored up
for the righteous.

23 The field of the poor yields abundant food,
but without justice, it is swept away.

24 The one who will not use the rod hates his son,
but the one who loves him disciplines
him diligently.

25 A righteous man eats until he is satisfied,
but the stomach of the wicked is empty.

14 Every wise woman builds her house,
but a foolish one tears it down
with her own hands.

2 Whoever lives with integrity fears the LORD,
but the one who is devious in his ways
despises Him.

3 The proud speech of a fool brings a rod
of discipline,
but the lips of the wise protect them.

4 Where there are no oxen, the feeding-trough
is empty,
but an abundant harvest comes
through the strength of an ox.

5 An honest witness does not deceive,
but a dishonest witness utters lies.

6 A mocker seeks wisdom and doesn't find it,
but knowledge comes easily to the perceptive.

7 Stay away from a foolish man;
you will gain no knowledge from his speech.

8 The sensible man's wisdom is to consider his way,
but the stupidity of fools deceives them.

9 Fools mock at making restitution,
but there is goodwill among the upright.

10 The heart knows its own bitterness,
and no outsider shares in its joy.

11 The house of the wicked will be destroyed,

but the tent of the upright will stand.

12 There is a way that seems right to a man,
but its end is the way to death.

13 Even in laughter a heart may be sad,
and joy may end in grief.

14 The disloyal will get what their conduct deserves,
and a good man, what his deeds deserve.

15 The inexperienced believe anything,
but the sensible watch their steps.

16 A wise man is cautious and turns from evil,
but a fool is easily angered and is careless.

17 A quick-tempered man acts foolishly,
and a man who schemes is hated.

18 The gullible inherit foolishness,
but the sensible are crowned with knowledge.

19 The evil bow before those who are good,
the wicked, at the gates of the righteous.

20 A poor man is hated even by his neighbor,
but there are many who love the rich.

21 The one who despises his neighbor sins,
but whoever shows kindness to the poor
will be happy.

22 Don't those who plan evil go astray?
But those who plan good find loyalty
and faithfulness.

23 There is profit in all hard work,
but endless talk leads only to poverty.

24 The crown of the wise is their wealth,
but the foolishness of fools produces foolishness.

25 A truthful witness rescues lives,
but one who utters lies is deceitful.

26 In the fear of the LORD one has strong confidence

and his children have a refuge.

27 The fear of the LORD is a fountain of life,
turning people from the snares of death.

28 A large population is a king's splendor,
but a shortage of people is a ruler's devastation.

29 A patient person shows great understanding,
but a quick-tempered one promotes foolishness.

30 A tranquil heart is life to the body,
but jealousy is rottenness to the bones.

31 The one who oppresses the poor insults
their Maker,
but one who is kind to the needy honors Him.

32 The wicked are thrown down by their own sin,
but the righteous have a refuge when they die.

33 Wisdom resides in the heart of the discerning;
she is known even among fools.

34 Righteousness exalts a nation,
but sin is a disgrace to any people.

35 A king favors a wise servant,
but his anger falls on a disgraceful one.

15

A gentle answer turns away anger,
but a harsh word stirs up wrath.

2 The tongue of the wise
makes knowledge attractive,
but the mouth of fools blurts out foolishness.

3 The eyes of the LORD are everywhere,
observing the wicked and the good.

4 The tongue that heals is a tree of life,
but a devious tongue breaks the spirit.

5 A fool despises his father's instruction,
but a person who heeds correction is sensible.

6 The house of the righteous has great wealth,

but trouble accompanies the income of the wicked.

7   The lips of the wise broadcast knowledge,
but not so the heart of fools.

8   The sacrifice of the wicked is detestable
to the Lord,
but the prayer of the upright is His delight.

9   The Lord detests the way of the wicked,
but He loves the one who pursues righteousness.

10 Discipline is harsh for the one who leaves the path;
the one who hates correction will die.

11 Sheol and Abaddon lie open before the Lord—
how much more, human hearts.

12 A mocker doesn't love one who corrects him;
he will not consult the wise.

13 A joyful heart makes a face cheerful,
but a sad heart produces a broken spirit.

14 A discerning mind seeks knowledge,
but the mouth of fools feeds on foolishness.

15 All the days of the oppressed are miserable,
but a cheerful heart has a continual feast.

16 Better a little with the fear of the Lord
than great treasure with turmoil.

17 Better a meal of vegetables where there is love
than a fattened calf with hatred.

18 A hot-tempered man stirs up conflict,
but a man slow to anger calms strife.

19 A slacker's way is like a thorny hedge,
but the path of the upright is a highway.

20 A wise son brings joy to his father,
but a foolish one despises his mother.

21 Foolishness brings joy to one without sense,
but a man with understanding walks

a straight path.

22 Plans fail when there is no counsel,
but with many advisers they succeed.

23 A man takes joy in giving an answer;
and a timely word—how good that is!

24 For the discerning the path of life leads upward,
so that he may avoid going down to Sheol.

25 The LORD destroys the house of the proud,
but He protects the widow's territory.

26 The LORD detests the plans of an evil man,
but pleasant words are pure.

27 The one who profits dishonestly troubles
his household,
but the one who hates bribes will live.

28 The mind of the righteous person thinks
before answering,
but the mouth of the wicked blurts out evil things.

29 The LORD is far from the wicked,
but He hears the prayer of the righteous.

30 Bright eyes cheer the heart;
good news strengthens the bones.

31 An ear that listens to life-giving rebukes
will be at home among the wise.

32 Anyone who ignores instruction despises himself,
but whoever listens to correction acquires
good sense.

33 The fear of the LORD is wisdom's instruction,
and humility comes before honor.

16 The reflections of the heart belong to man,
but the answer of the tongue is from the LORD.

2 All a man's ways seem right in his own eyes,
but the LORD weighs the motives.

3   Commit your activities to the LORD
    and your plans will be achieved.

4   The LORD has prepared everything
    for His purpose—
    even the wicked for the day of disaster.

5   Everyone with a proud heart is detestable
    to the LORD;
    be assured, he will not go unpunished.

6   Wickedness is atoned for by loyalty
    and faithfulness,
    and one turns from evil by the fear of the LORD.

7   When a man's ways please the LORD,
    He makes even his enemies to be at peace
    with him.

8   Better a little with righteousness
    than great income with injustice.

9   A man's heart plans his way,
    but the LORD determines his steps.

10 God's verdict is on the lips of a king;
    his mouth should not err in judgment.

11 Honest balances and scales are the LORD's;
    all the weights in the bag are His concern.

12 Wicked behavior is detestable to kings,
    since a throne is established through righteousness.

13 Righteous lips are a king's delight,
    and he loves one who speaks honestly.

14 A king's fury is a messenger of death,
    but a wise man appeases it.

15 When a king's face lights up, there is life;
    his favor is like a cloud with spring rain.

16 Acquire wisdom—
    how much better it is than gold!
    And acquire understanding—

it is preferable to silver.

17 The highway of the upright avoids evil;
the one who guards his way protects his life.

18 Pride comes before destruction,
and an arrogant spirit before a fall.

19 Better to be lowly of spirit with the humble
than to divide plunder with the proud.

20 The one who understands a matter finds success,
and the one who trusts in the LORD will be happy.

21 Anyone with a wise heart is called discerning,
and pleasant speech increases learning.

22 Insight is a fountain of life for its possessor,
but folly is the instruction of fools.

23 A wise heart instructs its mouth
and increases learning with its speech.

24 Pleasant words are a honeycomb:
sweet to the taste and health to the body.

25 There is a way that seems right to a man,
but in the end it is the way of death.

26 A worker's appetite works for him
because his hunger urges him on.

27 A worthless man digs up evil,
and his speech is like a scorching fire.

28 A contrary man spreads conflict,
and a gossip separates friends.

29 A violent man lures his neighbor,
leading him in a way that is not good.

30 The one who narrows his eyes
is planning deceptions;
the one who compresses his lips brings about evil.

31 Gray hair is a glorious crown;
it is found in the way of righteousness.

³² Patience is better than power,
and controlling one's temper, than capturing a city.

³³ The lot is cast into the lap,
but its every decision is from the LORD.

17 Better a dry crust with peace
than a house full of feasting with strife.

² A wise servant will rule over a disgraceful son
and share an inheritance among brothers.

³ A crucible is for silver and a smelter for gold,
but the LORD is a tester of hearts.

⁴ A wicked person listens to malicious talk;
a liar pays attention to a destructive tongue.

⁵ The one who mocks the poor insults his Maker,
and one who rejoices over disaster
will not go unpunished.

⁶ Grandchildren are the crown of the elderly,
and the pride of sons is their fathers.

⁷ Excessive speech is not appropriate on a fool's lips;
how much worse are lies for a ruler.

⁸ A bribe seems like a magic stone to its owner;
wherever he turns, he succeeds.

⁹ Whoever conceals an offense promotes love,
but whoever gossips about it separates friends.

¹⁰ A rebuke cuts into a perceptive person
more than a hundred lashes into a fool.

¹¹ An evil man seeks only rebellion;
a cruel messenger will be sent against him.

¹² Better for a man to meet a bear robbed of her cubs
than a fool in his foolishness.

¹³ If anyone returns evil for good,
evil will never depart from his house.

¹⁴ To start a conflict is to release a flood;

stop the dispute before it breaks out.

15 Acquitting the guilty and condemning the just—
both are detestable to the LORD.

16 Why does a fool have money in his hand
with no intention of buying wisdom?

17 A friend loves at all times,
and a brother is born for a difficult time.

18 One without sense enters an agreement
and puts up security for his friend.

19 One who loves to offend loves strife;
one who builds a high threshold invites injury.

20 One with a twisted mind will not succeed,
and one with deceitful speech will fall into ruin.

21 A man fathers a fool to his own sorrow;
the father of a fool has no joy.

22 A joyful heart is good medicine,
but a broken spirit dries up the bones.

23 A wicked man secretly takes a bribe
to subvert the course of justice.

24 Wisdom is the focus of the perceptive,
but a fool's eyes roam to the ends of the earth.

25 A foolish son is grief to his father
and bitterness to the one who bore him.

26 It is certainly not good to fine an innocent person,
or to beat a noble for his honesty.

27 The intelligent person restrains his words,
and one who keeps a cool head
is a man of understanding.

28 Even a fool is considered wise
when he keeps silent,
discerning, when he seals his lips.

18 One who isolates himself pursues selfish desires;

he rebels against all sound judgment.

2   A fool does not delight in understanding,
but only wants to show off his opinions.

3   When a wicked man comes, shame does also,
and along with dishonor, disgrace.

4   The words of a man's mouth are deep waters,
a flowing river, a fountain of wisdom.

5   It is not good to show partiality to the guilty
by perverting the justice due the innocent.

6   A fool's lips lead to strife,
and his mouth provokes a beating.

7   A fool's mouth is his devastation,
and his lips are a trap for his life.

8   A gossip's words are like choice food
that goes down to one's innermost being.

9   The one who is truly lazy in his work
is brother to a vandal.

10   The name of the LORD is a strong tower;
the righteous run to it and are protected.

11   A rich man's wealth is his fortified city;
in his imagination it is like a high wall.

12   Before his downfall a man's heart is proud,
but before honor comes humility.

13   The one who gives an answer before he listens—
this is foolishness and disgrace for him.

14   A man's spirit can endure sickness,
but who can survive a broken spirit?

15   The mind of the discerning acquires knowledge,
and the ear of the wise seeks it.

16   A gift opens doors for a man
and brings him before the great.

17   The first to state his case seems right

until another comes and cross-examines him.

18 Casting the lot ends quarrels
and separates powerful opponents.

19 An offended brother is harder to reach
than a fortified city,
and quarrels are like the bars of a fortress.

20 From the fruit of his mouth a man's stomach
is satisfied;
he is filled with the product of his lips.

21 Life and death are in the power of the tongue,
and those who love it will eat its fruit.

22 A man who finds a wife finds a good thing
and obtains favor from the LORD.

23 The poor man pleads,
but the rich one answers roughly.

24 A man with many friends may be harmed,
but there is a friend who stays closer
than a brother.

19 Better a poor man who walks in integrity
than someone who has deceitful lips and is a fool.

2 Even zeal is not good without knowledge,
and the one who acts hastily sins.

3 A man's own foolishness leads him astray,
yet his heart rages against the LORD.

4 Wealth attracts many friends,
but a poor man is separated from his friend.

5 A false witness will not go unpunished,
and one who utters lies will not escape.

6 Many seek the favor of a ruler,
and everyone is a friend of one who gives gifts.

7 All the brothers of a poor man hate him;
how much more do his friends

keep their distance from him!
He may pursue them with words,
but they are not there.

8 The one who acquires good sense loves himself;
one who safeguards understanding finds success.

9 A false witness will not go unpunished,
and one who utters lies perishes.

10 Luxury is not appropriate for a fool—
how much less for a slave to rule over princes!

11 A person's insight gives him patience,
and his virtue is to overlook an offense.

12 A king's rage is like a lion's roar,
but his favor is like dew on the grass.

13 A foolish son is his father's ruin,
and a wife's nagging is an endless dripping.

14 A house and wealth are inherited from fathers,
but a sensible wife is from the LORD.

15 Laziness induces deep sleep,
and a lazy person will go hungry.

16 The one who keeps commands preserves himself;
one who disregards his ways will die.

17 Kindness to the poor is a loan to the LORD,
and He will give a reward to the lender.

18 Discipline your son while there is hope;
don't be intent on killing him.

19 A person with great anger bears the penalty;
if you rescue him, you'll have to do it again.

20 Listen to counsel and receive instruction
so that you may be wise in later life.

21 Many plans are in a man's heart,
but the LORD's decree will prevail.

22 A man's desire should be loyalty to the covenant;

better to be a poor man than a perjurer.

23 The fear of the LORD leads to life;
one will sleep at night without danger.

24 The slacker buries his hand in the bowl;
he doesn't even bring it back to his mouth.

25 Strike a mocker, and the inexperienced learn
a lesson;
rebuke the discerning, and he gains knowledge.

26 The one who assaults his father and evicts
his mother
is a disgraceful and shameful son.

27 If you stop listening to instruction, my son,
you will stray from the words of knowledge.

28 A worthless witness mocks justice,
and a wicked mouth swallows iniquity.

29 Judgments are prepared for mockers,
and beatings for the backs of fools.

20 Wine is a mocker, beer is a brawler,
and whoever staggers because of them is not wise.

2 A king's terrible wrath is like the roaring of a lion;
anyone who provokes him endangers himself.

3 It is honorable for a man to resolve a dispute,
but any fool can get himself into a quarrel.

4 The slacker does not plow during planting season;
at harvest time he looks, and there is nothing.

5 Counsel in a man's heart is deep water;
but a man of understanding draws it up.

6 Many a man proclaims his own loyalty,
but who can find a trustworthy man?

7 The one who lives with integrity is righteous;
his children who come after him will be happy.

8 A king sitting on a throne to judge

sifts out all evil with his eyes.

⁹ Who can say, "I have kept my heart pure;
I am cleansed from my sin"?

¹⁰ Differing weights and varying measures—
both are detestable to the Lᴏʀᴅ.

¹¹ Even a young man is known by his actions—
by whether his behavior is pure and upright.

¹² The hearing ear and the seeing eye—
the Lᴏʀᴅ made them both.

¹³ Don't love sleep, or you will become poor;
open your eyes, and you'll have enough to eat.

¹⁴ "It's worthless, it's worthless!" the buyer says,
but after he is on his way, he gloats.

¹⁵ There is gold and a multitude of jewels,
but knowledgeable lips are a rare treasure.

¹⁶ Take his garment,
for he has put up security for a stranger;
get collateral if it is for foreigners.

¹⁷ Food gained by fraud is sweet to a man,
but afterwards his mouth is full of gravel.

¹⁸ Finalize plans through counsel,
and wage war with sound guidance.

¹⁹ The one who reveals secrets is a constant gossip;
avoid someone with a big mouth.

²⁰ Whoever curses his father or mother—
his lamp will go out in deep darkness.

²¹ An inheritance gained prematurely
will not be blessed ultimately.

²² Don't say, "I will avenge this evil!"
Wait on the Lᴏʀᴅ, and He will rescue you.

²³ Differing weights are detestable to the Lᴏʀᴅ,
and dishonest scales are unfair.

24   A man's steps are determined by the LORD,
      so how can anyone understand his own way?

25   It is a trap for anyone to dedicate something rashly
      and later to reconsider his vows.

26   A wise king separates out the wicked
      and drives the threshing wheel over them.

27   A person's breath is the lamp of the LORD,
      searching the innermost parts.

28   Loyalty and faithfulness deliver a king;
      through loyalty he maintains his throne.

29   The glory of young men is their strength,
      and the splendor of old men is gray hair.

30   Lashes and wounds purge away evil,
      and beatings cleanse the innermost parts.

21

      A king's heart is a water channel
      in the LORD's hand:
      He directs it wherever He chooses.

2   All the ways of a man seem right to him,
      but the LORD evaluates the motives.

3   Doing what is righteous and just
      is more acceptable to the LORD than sacrifice.

4   The lamp that guides the wicked—
      haughty eyes and an arrogant heart—is sin.

5   The plans of the diligent certainly lead to profit,
      but anyone who is reckless only becomes poor.

6   Making a fortune through a lying tongue
      is a vanishing mist, a pursuit of death.

7   The violence of the wicked sweeps them away
      because they refuse to act justly.

8   A guilty man's conduct is crooked,
      but the behavior of the innocent is upright.

9   Better to live on the corner of a roof

than to share a house with a nagging wife.

10 A wicked person desires evil;
he has no consideration for his neighbor.

11 When a mocker is punished,
the inexperienced become wiser;
when one teaches a wise man,
he acquires knowledge.

12 The Righteous One considers the house
of the wicked;
He brings the wicked to ruin.

13 The one who shuts his ears to the cry of the poor
will himself also call out and not be answered.

14 A secret gift soothes anger,
and a covert bribe, fierce rage.

15 Justice executed is a joy to the righteous
but a terror to those who practice iniquity.

16 The man who strays from the way of wisdom
will come to rest
in the assembly of the departed spirits.

17 The one who loves pleasure will become
a poor man;
whoever loves wine and oil will not get rich.

18 The wicked are a ransom for the righteous,
and the treacherous, for the upright.

19 Better to live in a wilderness
than with a nagging and hot-tempered wife.

20 Precious treasure and oil are in the dwelling
of the wise,
but a foolish man consumes them.

21 The one who pursues righteousness
and faithful love
will find life, righteousness, and honor.

22 The wise conquer a city of warriors

and bring down its mighty fortress.

23 The one who guards his mouth and tongue
keeps himself out of trouble.

24 The proud and arrogant person, named "Mocker,"
acts with excessive pride.

25 A slacker's craving will kill him
because his hands refuse to work.

26 He is filled with craving all day long,
but the righteous give and don't hold back.

27 The sacrifice of a wicked person is detestable—
how much more so
when he brings it with ulterior motives!

28 A lying witness will perish,
but the one who listens will speak successfully.

29 A wicked man puts on a bold face,
but the upright man considers his way.

30 No wisdom, no understanding, and no counsel
will prevail against the LORD.

31 A horse is prepared for the day of battle,
but victory comes from the LORD.

22 A good name is to be chosen over great wealth;
favor is better than silver and gold.

2 The rich and the poor have this in common:
the LORD made them both.

3 A sensible person sees danger and takes cover,
but the inexperienced keep going
and are punished.

4 The result of humility is fear of the LORD,
along with wealth, honor, and life.

5 There are thorns and snares on the path
of the crooked;
the one who guards himself stays far from them.

⁶ Teach a youth about the way he should go;
even when he is old he will not depart from it.

⁷ The rich rule over the poor,
and the borrower is a slave to the lender.

⁸ The one who sows injustice will reap disaster,
and the rod of his fury will be destroyed.

⁹ A generous person will be blessed,
for he shares his food with the poor.

¹⁰ Drive out a mocker, and conflict goes too;
then lawsuits and dishonor will cease.

¹¹ The one who loves a pure heart
and gracious lips—the king is his friend.

¹² The LORD's eyes keep watch over knowledge,
but He overthrows the words of the treacherous.

¹³ The slacker says, "There's a lion outside!
I'll be killed in the streets!"

¹⁴ The mouth of the forbidden woman is a deep pit;
a man cursed by the LORD will fall into it.

¹⁵ Foolishness is tangled up in the heart of a youth;
the rod of discipline will drive it away from him.

¹⁶ Oppressing the poor to enrich oneself,
and giving to the rich—both lead only to poverty.

Words of the Wise

¹⁷ Listen closely, pay attention to the words
of the wise,
and apply your mind to my knowledge.

¹⁸ For it is pleasing if you keep them within you
and if they are constantly on your lips.

¹⁹ I have instructed you today—even you—
so that your confidence may be in the LORD.

²⁰ Haven't I written for you thirty sayings
about counsel and knowledge,

²¹ in order to teach you true and reliable words,
so that you may give a dependable report

to those who sent you?

22   Don't rob a poor man because he is poor,
      and don't crush the oppressed at the gate,
23   for the LORD will take up their case
      and will plunder those who plunder them.

24   Don't make friends with an angry man,
      and don't be a companion of a hot-tempered man,
25   or you will learn his ways
      and entangle yourself in a snare.

26   Don't be one of those who enter agreements,
      who put up security for loans.
27   If you have no money to pay,
      even your bed will be taken from under you.

28   Don't move an ancient property line
      that your fathers set up.

29   Do you see a man skilled in his work?
      He will stand in the presence of kings.
      He will not stand in the presence
      of unknown men.

23 When you sit down to dine with a ruler,
        consider carefully what is before you,
2   and stick a knife in your throat
        if you have a big appetite;
3   don't desire his choice food,
        for that food is deceptive.

4   Don't wear yourself out to get rich;
        stop giving your attention to it.
5   As soon as your eyes fly to it, it disappears,
        for it makes wings for itself
        and flies like an eagle to the sky.

6   Don't eat a stingy person's bread,
        and don't desire his choice food,
7   for as he thinks within himself, so he is.
        "Eat and drink," he says to you,
        but his heart is not with you.

⁸ You will vomit the little you've eaten
and waste your pleasant words.

⁹ Don't speak to a fool,
for he will despise the insight of your words.

¹⁰ Don't move an ancient property line,
and don't encroach on the fields of the fatherless,
¹¹ for their Redeemer is strong,
and He will take up their case against you.

¹² Apply yourself to instruction
and listen to words of knowledge.

¹³ Don't withhold correction from a youth;
if you beat him with a rod, he will not die.
¹⁴ Strike him with a rod,
and you will rescue his life from Sheol.

¹⁵ My son, if your heart is wise,
my heart will indeed rejoice.
¹⁶ My innermost being will cheer
when your lips say what is right.

¹⁷ Don't be jealous of sinners;
instead, always fear the LORD.
¹⁸ For then you will have a future,
and your hope will never fade.

¹⁹ Listen, my son, and be wise;
keep your mind on the right course.
²⁰ Don't associate with those who drink
too much wine,
or with those who gorge themselves on meat.
²¹ For the drunkard and the glutton will become poor,
and grogginess will clothe them in rags.

²² Listen to your father who gave you life,
and don't despise your mother when she is old.
²³ Buy—and do not sell—truth,
wisdom, instruction, and understanding.
²⁴ The father of a righteous son will rejoice greatly,
and one who fathers a wise son will delight in him.

25 Let your father and mother have joy,
and let her who gave birth to you rejoice.

26 My son, give me your heart,
and let your eyes observe my ways.

27 For a prostitute is a deep pit,
and a forbidden woman is a narrow well;

28 indeed, she sets an ambush like a robber
and increases those among men
who are unfaithful.

29 Who has woe? Who has sorrow?
Who has conflicts? Who has complaints?
Who has wounds for no reason?
Who has red eyes?

30 Those who linger over wine,
those who go looking for mixed wine.

31 Don't gaze at wine when it is red,
when it gleams in the cup
and goes down smoothly.

32 In the end it bites like a snake
and stings like a viper.

33 Your eyes will see strange things,
and you will say absurd things.

34 You'll be like someone sleeping out at sea
or lying down on the top of a ship's mast.

35 "They struck me, but I feel no pain!
They beat me, but I didn't know it!
When will I wake up?
I'll look for another drink."

24

Don't envy evil men
or desire to be with them,

2 for their hearts plan violence,
and their words stir up trouble.

3 A house is built by wisdom,
and it is established by understanding;

4 by knowledge the rooms are filled
with every precious and beautiful treasure.

⁵ A wise warrior is better than a strong one,
and a man of knowledge than one of strength;
⁶ for you should wage war with sound guidance—
victory comes with many counselors.

⁷ Wisdom is inaccessible to a fool;
he does not open his mouth at the gate.
⁸ The one who plots evil
will be called a schemer.
⁹ A foolish scheme is sin,
and a mocker is detestable to people.

¹⁰ If you do nothing in a difficult time,
your strength is limited.
¹¹ Rescue those being taken off to death,
and save those stumbling toward slaughter.
¹² If you say, "But we didn't know about this,"
won't He who weighs hearts consider it?
Won't He who protects your life know?
Won't He repay a person according to his work?

¹³ Eat honey, my son, for it is good,
and the honeycomb is sweet to your palate;
¹⁴ realize that wisdom is the same for you.
If you find it, you will have a future,
and your hope will never fade.

¹⁵ Don't set an ambush, wicked man,
at the camp of the righteous man;
don't destroy his dwelling.
¹⁶ Though a righteous man falls seven times,
he will get up,
but the wicked will stumble into ruin.

¹⁷ Don't gloat when your enemy falls,
and don't let your heart rejoice when he stumbles,
¹⁸ or the LORD will see, be displeased,
and turn His wrath away from him.

¹⁹ Don't worry because of evildoers,
and don't envy the wicked.
²⁰ For the evil have no future;

the lamp of the wicked will be put out.

21 My son, fear the LORD, as well as the king,
and don't associate with rebels,
22 for their destruction will come suddenly;
who knows what disaster these two can bring?

23 These sayings also belong to the wise:

It is not good to show partiality in judgment.
24 Whoever says to the guilty, "You are innocent"—
people will curse him, and tribes
will denounce him;
25 but it will go well with those who convict
the guilty,
and a generous blessing will come to them.

26 He who gives an honest answer
gives a kiss on the lips.

27 Complete your outdoor work, and prepare
your field;
afterwards, build your house.

28 Don't testify against your neighbor without cause.
Don't deceive with your lips.
29 Don't say, "I'll do to him what he did to me;
I'll repay the man for what he has done."

30 I went by the field of a slacker
and by the vineyard of a man lacking sense.
31 Thistles had come up everywhere,
weeds covered the ground,
and the stone wall was ruined.
32 I saw, and took it to heart;
I looked, and received instruction:
33 a little sleep, a little slumber,
a little folding of the arms to rest,
34 and your poverty will come like a robber,
your need, like a bandit.

25 These too are proverbs of Solomon,
which the men of Hezekiah, king of Judah, copied.

2 It is the glory of God to conceal a matter
and the glory of kings to investigate a matter.

3 As the heaven is high and the earth is deep,
so the hearts of kings cannot be investigated.

4 Remove impurities from silver,
and a vessel will be produced for a silversmith.

5 Remove the wicked from the king's presence,
and his throne will be established in righteousness.

6 Don't brag about yourself before the king,
and don't stand in the place of the great;

7 for it is better for him to say to you,
"Come up here!"
than to demote you in plain view of a noble.

8 Don't take a matter to court hastily.
Otherwise, what will you do afterwards
if your opponent humiliates you?

9 Make your case with your opponent
without revealing another's secret;

10 otherwise, the one who hears will disgrace you,
and you'll never live it down.

11 A word spoken at the right time
is like golden apples on a silver tray.

12 A wise correction to a receptive ear
is like a gold ring or an ornament of gold.

13 To those who send him, a trustworthy messenger
is like the coolness of snow on a harvest day;
he refreshes the life of his masters.

14 The man who boasts about a gift
that does not exist
is like clouds and wind without rain.

15 A ruler can be persuaded through patience,
and a gentle tongue can break a bone.

16   If you find honey, eat only what you need;
      otherwise, you'll get sick from it and vomit.
17   Seldom set foot in your neighbor's house;
      otherwise, he'll get sick of you and hate you.

18   A man giving false testimony against his neighbor
      is like a club, a sword, or a sharp arrow.
19   Trusting an unreliable person in a time of trouble
      is like a rotten tooth or a faltering foot.

20   Singing songs to a troubled heart
      is like taking off clothing on a cold day,
      or like pouring vinegar on soda.

21   If your enemy is hungry, give him food to eat,
      and if he is thirsty, give him water to drink;
22   for you will heap coals on his head,
      and the LORD will reward you.

23   The north wind produces rain,
      and a backbiting tongue, angry looks.
24   Better to live on the corner of a roof
      than in a house shared with a nagging wife.
25   Good news from a distant land
      is like cold water to a parched throat.
26   A righteous person who yields to the wicked
      is like a muddied spring or a polluted well.
27   It is not good to eat too much honey,
      or to seek glory after glory.
28   A man who does not control his temper
      is like a city whose wall is broken down.

26   Like snow in summer and rain at harvest,
      honor is inappropriate for a fool.
2   Like a flitting sparrow or a fluttering swallow,
      an undeserved curse goes nowhere.
3   A whip for the horse, a bridle for the donkey,
      and a rod for the backs of fools.
4   Don't answer a fool according to his foolishness,
      or you'll be like him yourself.
5   Answer a fool according to his foolishness,

or he'll become wise in his own eyes.

6 The one who sends a message by a fool's hand
cuts off his own feet and drinks violence.

7 A proverb in the mouth of a fool
is like lame legs that hang limp.

8 Giving honor to a fool
is like binding a stone in a sling.

9 A proverb in the mouth of a fool
is like a stick with thorns,
brandished by the hand of a drunkard.

10 The one who hires a fool, or who hires
those passing by,
is like an archer who wounds everyone.

11 As a dog returns to its vomit,
so a fool repeats his foolishness.

12 Do you see a man who is wise in his own eyes?
There is more hope for a fool than for him.

13 The slacker says, "There's a lion in the road—
a lion in the public square!"

14 A door turns on its hinge,
and a slacker, on his bed.

15 The slacker buries his hand in the bowl;
he is too weary to bring it to his mouth.

16 In his own eyes, a slacker is wiser
than seven men who can answer sensibly.

17 A passerby who meddles in a quarrel that's not his
is like one who grabs a dog by the ears.

18 Like a madman who throws flaming darts
and deadly arrows,

19 so is the man who deceives his neighbor
and says, "I was only joking!"

20 Without wood, fire goes out;
without a gossip, conflict dies down.

21 As charcoal for embers and wood for fire,
so is a quarrelsome man for kindling strife.

22 A gossip's words are like choice food
that goes down to one's innermost being.

23 Smooth lips with an evil heart
are like glaze on an earthen vessel.

24 A hateful person disguises himself with his speech
and harbors deceit within.

25 When he speaks graciously, don't believe him,
for there are seven abominations in his heart.

26 Though his hatred is concealed by deception,
his evil will be revealed in the assembly.

27 The one who digs a pit will fall into it,
and whoever rolls a stone—
it will come back on him.

28 A lying tongue hates those it crushes,
and a flattering mouth causes ruin.

27 Don't boast about tomorrow,
for you don't know what a day might bring.

2 Let another praise you, and not your own mouth—
a stranger, and not your own lips.

3 A stone is heavy and sand, a burden,
but aggravation from a fool outweighs them both.

4 Fury is cruel, and anger is a flood,
but who can withstand jealousy?

5 Better an open reprimand
than concealed love.

6 The wounds of a friend are trustworthy,
but the kisses of an enemy are excessive.

7 A person who is full tramples on a honeycomb,
but to a hungry person, any bitter thing is sweet.

8 A man wandering from his home
is like a bird wandering from its nest.

9 Oil and incense bring joy to the heart,
and the sweetness of a friend is better than self-counsel.

10 Don't abandon your friend or your father's friend,
and don't go to your brother's house

in your time of calamity;
better a neighbor nearby than a brother far away.

11 Be wise, my son, and bring my heart joy,
so that I can answer anyone who taunts me.

12 The sensible see danger and take cover;
the foolish keep going and are punished.

13 Take his garment,
for he has put up security for a stranger;
get collateral if it is for foreigners.

14 If one blesses his neighbor
with a loud voice early in the morning,
it will be counted as a curse to him.

15 An endless dripping on a rainy day
and a nagging wife are alike.

16 The one who controls her controls the wind
and grasps oil with his right hand.

17 Iron sharpens iron,
and one man sharpens another.

18 Whoever tends a fig tree will eat its fruit,
and whoever looks after his master
will be honored.

19 As the water reflects the face,
so the heart reflects the person.

20 Sheol and Abaddon are never satisfied,
and people's eyes are never satisfied.

21 Silver is tested in a crucible, gold in a smelter,
and a man, by the praise he receives.

22 Though you grind a fool
in a mortar with a pestle along with grain,
you will not separate his foolishness from him.

23 Know well the condition of your flock,
and pay attention to your herds,
24 for wealth is not forever;

not even a crown lasts for all time.

25 When hay is removed and new growth appears
and the grain from the hills is gathered in,

26 lambs will provide your clothing,
and goats, the price of a field;

27 there will be enough goat's milk for your food—
food for your household and nourishment
for your servants.

28

The wicked flee when no one is pursuing them,
but the righteous are as bold as a lion.

2 When a land is in rebellion, it has many rulers,
but with a discerning and knowledgeable person,
it endures.

3 A destitute leader who oppresses the poor
is like a driving rain that leaves no food.

4 Those who reject the law praise the wicked,
but those who keep the law battle against them.

5 Evil men do not understand justice,
but those who seek the LORD
understand everything.

6 Better a poor man who lives with integrity
than a rich man who distorts right and wrong.

7 A discerning son keeps the law,
but a companion of gluttons humiliates his father.

8 Whoever increases his wealth
through excessive interest
collects it for one who is kind to the poor.

9 Anyone who turns his ear away from hearing
the law—
even his prayer is detestable.

10 The one who leads the upright into an evil way
will fall into his own pit,
but the blameless will inherit what is good.

11   A rich man is wise in his own eyes,
but a poor man who has discernment
sees through him.

12   When the righteous triumph,
there is great rejoicing,
but when the wicked come to power,
people hide themselves.

13   The one who conceals his sins
will not prosper,
but whoever confesses and renounces them
will find mercy.

14   Happy is the one who is always reverent,
but one who hardens his heart falls into trouble.

15   A wicked ruler over a helpless people
is like a roaring lion or a charging bear.

16   A leader who lacks understanding
is very oppressive,
but one who hates unjust gain
prolongs his life.

17   A man burdened by bloodguilt
will be a fugitive until death.
Let no one help him.

18   The one who lives with integrity will be helped,
but one who distorts right and wrong
will suddenly fall.

19   The one who works his land
will have plenty of food,
but whoever chases fantasies
will have his fill of poverty.

20   A faithful man will have many blessings,
but one in a hurry to get rich
will not go unpunished.

21   It is not good to show partiality—
yet a man may sin for a piece of bread.

22   A greedy man is in a hurry for wealth;
he doesn't know that poverty will come to him.

23   One who rebukes a person will later find
more favor
than one who flatters with his tongue.

24   The one who robs his father or mother
and says, "That's no sin,"
is a companion to a man who destroys.

25   A greedy person provokes conflict,
but whoever trusts in the LORD will prosper.

26   The one who trusts in himself is a fool,
but one who walks in wisdom will be safe.

27   The one who gives to the poor
will not be in need,
but one who turns his eyes away
will receive many curses.

28   When the wicked come to power,
people hide,
but when they are destroyed,
the righteous flourish.

29

One who becomes stiff-necked,
after many reprimands
will be broken suddenly—
and without a remedy.

2   When the righteous flourish, the people rejoice,
but when the wicked rule, people groan.

3   A man who loves wisdom brings joy to his father,
but one who consorts with prostitutes destroys
his wealth.

4   By justice a king brings stability to a land,
but a man who demands "contributions"
demolishes it.

5   A man who flatters his neighbor

spreads a net for his feet.

6 An evil man is caught by sin,
but the righteous one sings and rejoices.

7 The righteous person knows the rights of the poor,
but the wicked one does not understand
these concerns.

8 Mockers inflame a city,
but the wise turn away anger.

9 If a wise man goes to court with a fool,
there will be ranting and raving but no resolution.

10 Bloodthirsty men hate an honest person,
but the upright care about him.

11 A fool gives full vent to his anger,
but a wise man holds it in check.

12 If a ruler listens to lies,
all his servants will be wicked.

13 The poor and the oppressor have this in common:
the LORD gives light to the eyes of both.

14 A king who judges the poor with fairness—
his throne will be established forever.

15 A rod of correction imparts wisdom,
but a youth left to himself
is a disgrace to his mother.

16 When the wicked increase, rebellion increases,
but the righteous will see their downfall.

17 Discipline your son, and he will give you comfort;
he will also give you delight.

18 Without revelation people run wild,
but one who keeps the law will be happy.

19 A servant cannot be disciplined by words;
though he understands, he doesn't respond.

20 Do you see a man who speaks too soon?

There is more hope for a fool than for him.

21 A slave pampered from his youth
will become arrogant later on.

22 An angry man stirs up conflict,
and a hot-tempered man increases rebellion.

23 A person's pride will humble him,
but a humble spirit will gain honor.

24 To be a thief's partner is to hate oneself;
he hears the curse but will not testify.

25 The fear of man is a snare,
but the one who trusts in the LORD is protected.

26 Many seek a ruler's favor,
but a man receives justice from the LORD.

27 An unjust man is detestable to the righteous,
and one whose way is upright
is detestable to the wicked.

The Words of Agur

30 The words of Agur son of Jakeh. The oracle.

The man's oration to Ithiel, to Ithiel and Ucal:

2 I am the least intelligent of men,
and I lack man's ability to understand.

3 I have not gained wisdom,
and I have no knowledge of the Holy One.

4 Who has gone up to heaven and come down?
Who has gathered the wind in His hands?
Who has bound up the waters in a cloak?
Who has established all the ends of the earth?
What is His name,
and what is the name of His Son—
if you know?

5 Every word of God is pure;
He is a shield to those who take refuge in Him.

6 Don't add to His words,

or He will rebuke you, and you will be proved
a liar.

7   Two things I ask of You;
don't deny them to me before I die:

8   Keep falsehood and deceitful words far from me.
Give me neither poverty nor wealth;
feed me with the food I need.

9   Otherwise, I might have too much
and deny You, saying, "Who is the LORD?"
or I might have nothing and steal,
profaning the name of my God.

10   Don't slander a servant to his master,
or he will curse you, and you will become guilty.

11   There is a generation that curses its father
and does not bless its mother.

12   There is a generation that is pure in its own eyes,
yet is not washed from its filth.

13   There is a generation—how haughty its eyes
and pretentious its looks.

14   There is a generation whose teeth are swords,
whose fangs are knives,
devouring the oppressed from the land
and the needy from among mankind.

15   The leech has two daughters: Give, Give.
Three things are never satisfied;
four never say, "Enough!":

16   Sheol; a barren womb;
earth, which is never satisfied with water;
and fire, which never says, "Enough!"

17   As for the eye that ridicules a father
and despises obedience to a mother,
may ravens of the valley pluck it out
and young vultures eat it.

18   Three things are beyond me;
four I can't understand:

19   the way of an eagle in the sky,

the way of a snake on a rock,
the way of a ship at sea,
and the way of a man with a young woman.

20 This is the way of an adulteress:
she eats and wipes her mouth
and says, "I've done nothing wrong."

21 The earth trembles under three things;
it cannot bear up under four:
22 a servant when he becomes king,
a fool when he is stuffed with food,
23 an unloved woman when she marries,
and a serving girl when she ousts her lady.

24 Four things on earth are small,
yet they are extremely wise:
25 the ants are not a strong people,
yet they store up their food in the summer;
26 hyraxes are not a mighty people,
yet they make their homes in the cliffs;
27 locusts have no king,
yet all of them march in ranks;
28 a lizard can be caught in your hands,
yet it lives in kings' palaces.

29 Three things are stately in their stride,
even four are stately in their walk:
30 a lion, which is mightiest among beasts
and doesn't retreat before anything,
31 a strutting rooster, a goat,
and a king at the head of his army.

32 If you have been foolish by exalting yourself,
or if you've been scheming,
put your hand over your mouth.
33 For the churning of milk produces butter,
and twisting a nose draws blood,
and stirring up anger produces strife.

The Words of Lemuel

31 The words of King Lemuel,
   an oracle that his mother taught him:

2   What should I say, my son?
   What, son of my womb?
   What, son of my vows?

3   Don't spend your energy on women
   or your efforts on those who destroy kings.

4   It is not for kings, Lemuel,
   it is not for kings to drink wine
   or for rulers to desire beer.

5   Otherwise, they will drink,
   forget what is decreed,
   and pervert justice for all the oppressed.

6   Give beer to one who is dying,
   and wine to one whose life is bitter.

7   Let him drink so that he can forget his poverty
   and remember his trouble no more.

8   Speak up for those who have no voice,
   for the justice of all who are dispossessed.

9   Speak up, judge righteously,
   and defend the cause of the oppressed and needy.

In Praise of a Capable Wife

10   Who can find a capable wife?
   She is far more precious than jewels.

11   The heart of her husband trusts in her,
   and he will not lack anything good.

12   She rewards him with good, not evil,
   all the days of her life.

13   She selects wool and flax
   and works with willing hands.

14   She is like the merchant ships,
   bringing her food from far away.

15   She rises while it is still night
   and provides food for her household
   and portions for her servants.

16 She evaluates a field and buys it;
she plants a vineyard with her earnings.

17 She draws on her strength
and reveals that her arms are strong.

18 She sees that her profits are good,
and her lamp never goes out at night.

19 She extends her hands to the spinning staff,
and her hands hold the spindle.

20 Her hands reach out to the poor,
and she extends her hands to the needy.

21 She is not afraid for her household when it snows,
for all in her household are doubly clothed.

22 She makes her own bed coverings;
her clothing is fine linen and purple.

23 Her husband is known at the city gates,
where he sits among the elders of the land.

24 She makes and sells linen garments;
she delivers belts to the merchants.

25 Strength and honor are her clothing,
and she can laugh at the time to come.

26 She opens her mouth with wisdom,
and loving instruction is on her tongue.

27 She watches over the activities of her household
and is never idle.

28 Her sons rise up and call her blessed.
Her husband also praises her:

29 "Many women are capable,
but you surpass them all!"

30 Charm is deceptive and beauty is fleeting,
but a woman who fears the Lord will be praised.

31 Give her the reward of her labor,
and let her works praise her at the city gates.